Financial Integrity

God's Plan for Financial Freedom

Stan E. DeKoven

and

Steven M. Mills

Financial Integrity

God's Plan for Financial Freedom

Stan E. DeKoven and Steven M. Mills

Copyright © 2015 Stan E. DeKoven and Steven M. Mills

ISBN 978-1-61529-170-0

Published by Vision Publishing
1115 D Street
Ramona, CA 92065
1 800 9 VISION
www.booksbyvision.com

Table of Contents

Introduction

The subject of finances is mainly either neglected or abused in the church today. There are many believers who are living in financial bondage because they have been taught it is God's will for His people to be poor. Many proclaim it was God's will for them to be poor and if they tried to better themselves they would be going against God's will for their lives. This position is untrue and unbiblical, as we will soon see. At the same time there are believers living in bondage because they have been taught prosperity is a sign of faith. Thus, if you do not have an abundance of things then you are not spiritual. Consequently, people live above their means, often by going into debt, trying to keep up the appearance of prosperity. Even though they look prosperous to the outsider they are in financial bondage. These are the two extremes when dealing with finances. The truth is in the middle. It is the purpose of this book to bring a balanced Biblical view, leading to Financial Integrity.

> *3 John 2:2 Beloved, I pray that you may prosper in all things and be in health, just as your soul prospers.*

God is truly interested in our finances. The Lord is as interested in our financial prosperity and physical health as He is in our spiritual prosperity. Our financial situation hinges on the condition of our spiritual life and renewed mind. The flow of the blessings of God in our lives is in direct proportion to the health and prosperity of our soul (mind, emotions, will and heart). If you notice God's blessings are no longer flowing, as they once did, give yourself a spiritual checkup.

> *Genesis 3:17-18, Then to Adam He said, "Because you have listened to the voice of your wife, and have eaten from the tree about which I commanded you, saying, 'You shall not eat from it'; Cursed is the ground because of you; In toil you will eat of it all the days of your life. "Both thorns*

and thistles it shall grow for you, and you will eat the plants of the field;

Sin had a dramatic effect on man's provision. Before the fall of man, God met every need man had. As a result of the fall of man, God placed a curse upon the earth. We still struggle with that curse every time we go to work in the field or pull a weed from our garden. We are reminded of the curse placed on the earth each time we sweat at work.

1 Timothy 6:6 – 8, But godliness actually is a means of great gain when accompanied by contentment. For we have brought nothing into the world, so we cannot take anything out of it either. If we have food and covering, with these we shall be content.

Philippians 4:11 – 13, Not that I speak from want, for I have learned to be content in whatever circumstances I am. I know how to get along with humble means, and I also know how to live in prosperity; in any and every circumstance I have learned the secret of being filled and going hungry, both of having abundance and suffering need. I can do all things through Him who strengthens me.

God's desire is for His people to be content with what they have. The greatest question is not how much we have, but are we content with what we have? The key to godliness is contentment. The Apostle Paul said he was content in whatever state he found himself in. He was content when he was poor and he was content when he was rich. Paul's secret to his contentment was not based on material things but on his relationship with God.

1 Timothy 6:17 – 19, Instruct those who are rich in this present world not to be conceited or to fix their hope on the uncertainty of riches, but on God, who richly supplies us with all things to enjoy. Instruct them to do good, to be rich in good works, to be generous and ready to share, storing up for themselves the treasure of a good foundation for the

*future, so that they may take hold of that which is life
indeed.*

Ultimately God gives His people financial blessings for the
spreading of the Gospel to the nations. We are not blessed by God
to consume everything for ourselves. Yes, God has blessed us with
material things for our enjoyment. But, He also wants us to use the
blessings for His Work. We are to be ready to give and share with
those in need. A story about two seas in Galilee illustrates this
principle.

There are two seas in Galilee, the Sea of Galilee and the Dead Sea.
Both of them receive the fresh waters of the Jordan River. The Sea
of Galilee is a channel for the waters of the Jordan River. It gives
back to the Jordan what it receives. As a result it is full of life. On
the other hand the Dead Sea holds onto every drop of water it
receives, for it has no outlet. As a result, the water stays in the Dead
Sea, slowly evaporating, leaving only a high concentration of
minerals behind. Because the Dead Sea holds onto everything it
receives it produces death. It is the same way in our lives. God
desires for us to be a channel of His blessings to the whole world. If
you hold onto the blessings of God, they will stagnate and produce
death in your life. Which of the two Seas in Galilee do you want to
be like?

*2 Corinthians 8:7 – 9, But just as you abound in everything,
in faith and utterance and knowledge and in all earnestness
and in the love we inspired in you, see that you abound in
this gracious work also. I am not speaking this as a
command, but as proving through the earnestness of others
the sincerity of your love also. For you know the grace of
our Lord Jesus Christ, that though He was rich, yet for your
sake He became poor, so that you through His poverty
might become rich.*

Giving is a test of our love for God, We can always tell how much
we love God by the way we give. True love will always result in a
desire to give, God loved the world that he gave His only son. Jesus

loved us so much He gave up everything in heaven to come to earth to purchase our salvation by His death.

Luke 16:11 – 12, Therefore if you have not been faithful in the use of unrighteous wealth, who will entrust the true riches to you? And if you have not been faithful in the use of that which is another's, who will give you that which is your own?

Jesus taught the way we handle our money demonstrate how we handle other things God gives us responsibility over. Money is used to test our usefulness in the Kingdom of God. If we are faithful with possessions then God knows we will be faithful with the true riches of God (His Word, the Holy Spirit, the ministry, etc.) On the other hand, if we are unfaithful without money then we will be unfaithful with the things of God. Our Heavenly Father will never entrust the riches of the Kingdom of God to those who are unfaithful. There are churches around having all kinds of trouble because they are being run by men who are not faithful.

In each of our lives there are things which become blockades, or dams causing the blessings of God to either be hindered or stopped. These can be spiritual blockades or financial ones. In the book, Chapter One through Chapter Eight deals with General Principles and Spiritual Blockades. Chapter Nine through Chapter Sixteen deals with Financial Blockades. These Blockades are not arranged by order of priority but are simply in alphabetical order. It is impossible to prioritize them as each individual will have a different order to the Blockades in their lives.

After reading the Spiritual and Financial Blockades which can cause the flow of God's blessings to be hindered or stopped, we will cover Practical Advice and Observation about your finances. Chapters Seventeen through Twenty-One, you will find a series of teaching outlines about finances designed to help you further your studies on the subject Financial Integrity.

As you read through this book, ask the Holy Spirit to open the eyes of your understanding so you might see the truth about Financial Integrity.

If the Holy Spirit convicts you of one or several areas of your financial management, stop immediately and repent. Allow the Holy Spirit of God to shine the light of His Word in your heart showing any areas which are not pleasing to Him. We want God's blessing to have unimpeded flow in our lives.

A Prayer

Heavenly Father, I ask you to give to every reader the spirit of wisdom and revelation in the knowledge of Jesus Christ. Enlighten the eyes of their understanding so they may know the hope to which you have called them; so they may know the riches of their inheritance and may experience the exceeding greatness of your power. Father, allow them to see the reality of your place for their lives. May your anointing be upon these pages and upon the eyes of every reader!

In the name of Jesus, Amen.

Using This Book and Study Guide

This book and the companion study guide are designed for a student to learn the principles by distance education. However, it is most helpful to not just take the course but work through the principles found here with a disciple or mentor. To do this requires time and energy, so we encourage your disciple to do the following:

Read and prayerfully meditate on each lesson.

Look up each scripture reference and answer each question (a requirement for a student). They must learn to get into the Word and allow the Holy Spirit to teach them from the Word.

Schedule a regular time to meet with your disciple so you can share what you both have discovered from your individual study, and answer any questions which may arise from their time with the Lord. WARNING: do not preach at them or conduct a Bible Study class. This is a time for you to talk to them and nurture them in a very professional setting – like a parent to a child. Also, for the distance student, part of your assignment will be to use the book and study guide with discipline…so, get ready to work!

Mentors help your disciple to personally apply each lesson in a practical way. The Word is alive and must be activated in our everyday life if we are to see real transformation. Talk with them to make them be a part of the process for determining how they can live out what they have just discovered.

Encourage them to memorize the verse at the end of each lesson; both of you quote the verse when you meet together the next time.

A disciple must go beyond mere memorization and must be taught the art of biblical meditation. Demonstrate how to meditate, and encourage them to meditate daily on the scripture they are memorizing and the passages they are studying. (See Appendix I)

Instruct the disciple to keep a spiritual journal recording what God reveals to them in their personal study, as well as any fresh insight they may receive from their times of meditation. (See Appendix II)

Pray for them regularly, pray with them, and teach them to pray for you.

Encourage them to spend time with you, watch you, and walk with you. Remember: we are mentoring as an example – not becoming their pastor.

Assist your disciple in understanding the power of reproducing the life of Christ in others. Encouraging them to begin sharing their faith and edifying others with the truths they have been learning in the Word. The sooner they begin to share with others the more it becomes a part of them. (See Appendix III)

Stewardship

Chapter 1

Countless times over the past several years I (Dr. Stan) have heard someone in the church proclaim, "They are always taking offerings, pressuring me to give. All they want is my money!" Certainly, this sentiment is not a new one, and there are unfortunate cases where excessive and even exploitive emphasis on money and prosperity are practiced. However, the giving and receiving of money are only one part of the important topics of stewardship, which must be properly understood by the Christian church today.

They Just Want My Money

As mentioned above, I have heard countless times over the past several years someone in the church proclaim, "They are always taking offerings, pressuring me to give. All they want is my money!" Certainly, this sentiment is not a new one, and there are unfortunate cases where excessive and even exploitive emphasis on money and prosperity are practiced. However, the giving and receiving of money are only one part of the important topics of stewardship, which must be properly understood by the Christian church today. One thing is for certain, our prosperity is linked to our stewardship.

What Is Stewardship?

A steward is a person who manages the affairs of a household or an estate for an owner. As Christians, a steward is a manager of the affairs of God on earth, using the abilities, talents, and resources provided by the Lord to the best of one's ability.

Everything that one possesses, whether a gift or talent, has been received from the Lord. This includes time, talent, property, health, environment, relationships, and, of course, abundant life in the Kingdom of God. A Christian is given the wonderful privilege of serving and worshiping God through the gifts God has given. Giving back to God and managing the gifts he has given, with a heart of gratitude, is part of a believer's service to the Lord.

> *"As each one has received a special gift, employ it in serving one another as good stewards of the manifold grace of God"* *(1 Peter 4: 10).*

The Gift of Life

Of all gifts given by God, the first and greatest of all is life itself. A Christian's life is a sacred trust, and each believer is to give proper care for their life before God. The cavalier attitude of the world towards God's gift of human life is a modern tragedy. Life is a gift and is to be cared for and affirmed as good (Genesis 1).

God has provided to all the precious gift of life, yet no one knows the length of that life. Thus, stewardship must extend to the usage of time. The wise usage of time is essential to the enjoyment of life and the pleasing of the Lord. How does a believer balance their time? There are so many obstacles to balance. The possible distractions are innumerable because of modern life.

Certainly balance must be found within godly priorities: God first in prayer, praise, worship, and service; family second, in loving a spouse and nurturing the children; vocation third, providing for family and having something to give to those in need.

Health

One's health must be guarded, since the Lord desires all His children to enjoy long life and abundant health. As the Apostle John stated, "Beloved, I pray that in all respects you may prosper and be in good health, just as your soul prospers" (3 John 2).

Prosperity from John the apostle's view was both related to a vibrant soul (mind, will and emotions) in tune with Holy Spirit, and a healthy body, soul and spirit. These important things would be what ultimately helped a person fulfill the journey of life determined by

Father God. As I have stated many times, God wants us to have all we need for our journey, in terms of health and resources…but if you are not going anywhere, you probably don't need much…but if you are, you can trust God to provide what you need for the journey.

Talent

Many a Christian has stated with dismay, "I can't do anything. How could God use such a no talent like me?" The Word of God states in,

> *I Corinthians 12:12-20, For even as the body is one and yet has many members, and all the members of the body, though they are many, are one body, so also is Christ. For by one Spirit we were all baptized into one body, whether Jews or Greeks, whether slaves or free, and we were all made to drink of one Spirit.*
>
> *For the body is not one member, but many. If the foot says, "Because I am not a hand, I am not a part of the body," it is not for this reason any the less a part of the body. And if the ear says, "Because I am not an eye, I am not a part of the body," it is not for this reason any the less a part of the body. If the whole body were an eye, where would the hearing be? If the whole were hearing, where would the sense of smell be? But now God has placed the members, each one of them, in the body, just as He desired. If they were all one member, where would the body be? But now there are many members, but one body.*

The fact is, all of God's creation is a divine original, and all His children have natural and spiritual gifts needed for the kingdom of God. It may take some searching (most friends can tell you your talents), but once discovered, talents and abilities are to be submitted to the Lord for His purposes.

Christians do not have the option of idle observation of others' labor in the body of Christ. If we do not use the talents God has given us we may lose them. Part of the satisfaction of the Christian life is found in joyfully sharing one's talents with others.

Relationships

The Word of God states that the whole of God's requirements can be summarized in Matthew 22:37-39, *He said to him, "'YOU SHALL LOVE THE LORD YOUR GOD WITH ALL YOUR HEART, AND WITH ALL YOUR SOUL, AND WITH ALL YOUR MIND.' This is the great and foremost commandment. The second is like it, 'YOU SHALL LOVE YOUR NEIGHBOR AS YOURSELF.'"*

In fact, the requirement to love God and others unconditionally is not possible, outside of the grace of God living through us. Relationships are the building blocks of personality, self-image and a sense of worth. Christ affirms that to love God and our neighbor is our highest requirement, which can only be done through our relationship with Jesus Christ. All relationships are important, and by God's grace we can be good managers of our relationships as expressed in the key social arenas of life. These include:

- Home - Where a demonstration of God's love can be seen in our consideration of each other's needs, kindness towards each other, and faithfulness towards our family and self.
- Work - Where a true witness of God's grace can be demonstrated by our diligent work in service to the boss, whether he/she be a good boss or not.
- Church - Where the believers gather in vibrant worship and our gifts of love, friendship, and service can be practiced and celebrated.

Possessions

It is absolutely true that we brought nothing into this world, and we will take nothing out of it. All that we possess belongs to the Lord; we are merely stewards. As stewards, we have a responsibility to:

- Manage with care what God has given, not to hoard wealth, or hide talent, but use it for the expansion of the kingdom of God.
- Increase what God has given, for a good steward wants to show a profit for their labor, thus providing even more to give as God directs and provides for the next generation. ("Proverbs 13:22.)
- Share in the blessings of God through faithful, Holy Spirit led, generous, and systematic giving. It is in this last area that this article now places its emphasis, though all of these areas are important.

Generous Giving

It is a privilege to give. Of course, in these discussions, it is necessary to distinguish between giving and paying, to maintain clarity. In the Old Testament, the tithe belonged to God, so one paid their tithes. As New Testament believers, all our activity, including our giving, must be motivated by faith which works by love. A believer's heart, transformed by the Word of God, desires to give with generosity, not through compulsion.

A clear insight into giving is found in 2 Corinthians 16:2, where Paul says, "On the first day of every week, each one of you should set aside a sum of money in keeping with his income, saving it up so that when I come no collections will have to be made" (NIV).

From this is learned that giving is to be done on a regular weekly basis: "On the first day of every week." Then, Paul makes it very clear who is to participate. No believer is left out. It is all-inclusive: "each one of you." The method of giving is by earmarking a certain amount: "set aside" a percentage, "in keeping with your income." Here Paul gives the when, who, how and what of giving.

When?	Weekly (regularly) "on the first day of every week"
Who?	Inclusive (no believer left out) "each one of you"
How?	Earmarked "set aside"
What?	Percentage "in keeping with your income"

What about Tithing?

In the first place, tithing as part of the New Covenant is to be seen as a principle, not a law of giving to be feared, or to be used as a battering ram, forcing God's people to be good and give. Our giving should always be seen as returning to the Lord that which rightfully belongs to Him. This principle (which is a good starting point for many) designed by God is not a form of charity, but a beautiful means to establish God's people and His covenant.

One of the greatest joys of the Christian life is sharing. Deprive a person the privilege of supporting God's work and their happiness is taken from them. Generous giving of a tithe or more is one of the ways to grow and become stronger as Christians, for it is recognition of God's power.

Money is a physical means used by God to enhance spiritual growth. Whenever a Christian begins to trust the Lord for daily needs, spiritual growth will be the result. We are to be a people of faith instead of a people of fear whose anxiety level rises with one's needs.

When one gives of their finances generously, God blesses. When one withholds, they limit their own joy, for there is great joy in generous giving.

Giving is not only a holy habit, but a high honor. If all institutions, as well as individuals would begin to give generously, beginning with a tithe as a starting point, the church would have all it needs to fulfill the Great Commission.

Conclusion

God wants us to prosper…and prosperity, having all we need for our journey is linked to our soul, or our thinking, and a key component of our thinking is that all we have comes from God, all is his, he is good, and being generous demonstrates a heart truly set on God and his purposes.

Lesson One - Bribery

There are many scriptures in the Word of God which deal with the subject of bribery. This is one of the greatest blockades to financial freedom today. This cancer has gripped every area of society including the church. When I (Steve Mills) first arrived in Kenya I was given the job of obtaining a permit to show the Jesus film in one of the housing estates. Being new to the country I was ignorant of the way things were done in certain offices. After getting all the documentation which was needed I went to the appropriate office for the permit. I handed my paper to the man behind the desk who looked them over very carefully. He said, "Everything seems to be in order," then he just looked at me. Being new to this game and not knowing what was expected of me I looked back at him. For about five minutes we looked at each other and then the man said, "Come back tomorrow." On the third day it was the same story. While we were looking at each other another man came into the office for a permit. I noticed a couple large denomination bills of the local currency were sticking out of his paperwork. The man behind the desk put the money in his desk drawer and stamped the other man's papers and issued him a permit. Suddenly my eyes were opened and I understood what was expected of me if I wanted to get a permit. At this point I had a choice to make. Would I compromise my convictions and the Word of God or would I stand firm, not paying the bribe? If I had paid the bribe I could have gone to church on Sunday and praised God for the permit. The congregation would have given God the glory for the way He worked. No one would have known what I did but the man I gave the bribe to, God and myself. Sitting in that office I determined in my heart I would never pay a bribe even if it meant not getting the permit. For the next several weeks I was in that man's office every day. He got so tired of seeing me that he finally gave me the permit without the bribe. We must take a stand for what is right regardless of the cost. The church of the Lord Jesus must kill this cancer from our lives, churches, and nations.

The following comments and scriptures on bribery are by no means an exhaustive list but the most pointed and clearest references on the subject.

Exodus 23:8, "You shall not take a bribe, for a bribe blinds the clear-sighted and subverts the cause of the just.

God warned Israel against taking bribes because bribery causes spiritual blindness and perverts our word. If we engage in bribery, little by little our spiritual eyes are blind and our conscience is corrupted to the point that we no longer know the difference between right and wrong.

Deuteronomy 10:17, For the Lord your God is the God of gods and the Lord of lords, the great, the mighty, and the awesome God who does not show partiality nor take a bribe.

We, the children of God, are to be like our heavenly Father. God is not partial, and does not bribe nor can He be bribed. Children imitate what their parents do. Spend time in the presence of your Heavenly Father so you can learn what He is like. Jesus said He did nothing unless He first saw the Father do it (John 5:19). This scripture also hints that some people try to bribe God. You must ask, "How can a person try to bribe God?" There are many people who go to church on Sunday who have never accepted Jesus as their savior. As the offering plate comes by they drop money in hoping to bribe God into blessing them. Others are doing good works for the church as a bribe for God to let them into heaven without going through Jesus. There are still others who are in the ministry because surely God will have to let a Reverend into heaven. Remember what the scripture says, God does not take bribes.

Deuteronomy 16:19 – 20, You shall not distort justice; you shall not be partial, and you shall not take a bribe, for a bribe blinds the eyes of the wise and perverts the words of the righteous. Justice, and only justice, you shall pursue,

that you may live and possess the land which the Lord your
God is giving you.

Not only does bribery make us spiritually blind and twist our words, but it will keep us from inheriting what God has already given us. The effect of bribery haves eternal consequences, a matter of life and death. Our eternal destiny can be short circuited when we become involved in bribery.

> *Deuteronomy 27:25, 'Cursed is he who accepts a bribe to*
> *strike down an innocent person.' And all the people shall*
> *say, 'Amen.'*

Bribery will bring a curse, from God, upon those who are engaged in this activity.

> *1 Samuel 8:1 – 5, And it came about when Samuel was*
> *old that he appointed his sons judges over Israel. Now the*
> *name of his firstborn was Joel, and the name of his second,*
> *Abijah; they were judging in Beersheba. His sons,*
> *however, did not walk in his ways, but turned aside after*
> *dishonest gain and took bribes and perverted justice. Then*
> *all the elders of Israel gathered together and came to*
> *Samuel at Ramah; and they said to him, "Behold, you have*
> *grown old, and your sons do not walk in your ways. Now*
> *appoint a king for us to judge us like all the nations."*

When bribery is found in the leadership of the church it corrupts the ministry and causes the people of God to live in disobedience. The children of Israel demanded a king because the sons of Samuel were corrupt leaders. As a result of their corruption the people rejected God as their King. This was the beginning of the fall of the nation of Israel. When the leadership of the church becomes corrupt, engaging in bribery, it causes the people to turn their hearts from God.

> *2 Chronicles 19:7, Now then let the fear of the Lord be*
> *upon you; be very careful what you do, for the Lord our*

God will have no part in unrighteousness or partiality or the taking of a bribe."

Those involved in bribery do not walk in the fear of God. With the Lord there is no bribery. The fear of the Lord will direct us away from bribery and corruption.

Psalms 15 – 1, O Lord, who may abide in Your tent? Who may dwell on Your holy hill?

Bribery disqualifies a person from living deeply in the presence of the Lord. As we mentioned earlier, bribery has eternal consequences. Our eternal destination can be altered if we partake in bribery. Once I was helping a new church get their registration paperwork for the appeal. One day I saw the pastor and he was very excited, he showed me his registration. He had paid a bribe to a government official to get the registration. The simple act of bribery to get the church registered opened the door for the enemy to come in. Within a couple years the church was closed and the pastor was out of the ministry.

Psalms 26:9 – 10,   Do not take my soul away along with sinners, Nor my life with men of bloodshed, In whose hands is a wicked scheme, And whose right hand is full of bribes.

Everyone involved in bribery will be gathered together with sinners and blood thirsty men. Those engaged in bribery may gain something in this life but they will lose everything in *hell* for eternity. You must be careful never to get involved with bribery or you may find yourself spending a long, long time (like an eternity) with sinners.

Proverbs 17:23,   A wicked man receives a bribe from the bosom To pervert the ways of justice.

Bribery identifies a person as being wicked, and not interested in justice. It is sad to say but there are wicked people in the church. You will find people calling themselves Christians, giving or taking bribes. I have even heard missionaries justify themselves for paying bribes by saying, "It is the only way to get anything done in this country and God's work must go forth." God will not bless any work done for Him where bribery is involved. As soon as a bribe is given or taken the work ceases to be a work of God and becomes a work of the flesh.

Proverbs 29:4, The king gives stability to the land by justice, But a man who takes bribes overthrows it.

Bribery opens the door for all types of illegal practices which will destroy the economy of a nation. It is justice for all which will establish a nation before God. There is a reason the most corrupt nations in the world are among the poorest nations on earth.

Ecclesiastes 7:7, For oppression makes a wise man mad, And a bribe corrupts the heart.

The Hebrew word translated debased means to wander away or to perish. This verse is saying our heart will wander away from God or it will perish because of bribery. The Apostle John said in 1 John 3:20, 21 it is the heart of man which condemns him or shows he is righteous. Protect your heart. Have nothing to do with bribery.

Isaiah 1:23, Your rulers are rebels and companions of thieves; Everyone loves a bribe and chases after rewards. They do not defend the orphan, nor does the widow's plea come before them.

One of the signs of rebellion is bribery. Anyone involved with bribery is in rebellion against the government and to God. Bribery is against the law. If a person pays or accepts a bribe he has broken the law. Lawbreakers are in rebellion.

Isaiah 5:22 – 23, Woe to those who are heroes in drinking wine and valiant men in mixing strong drink, Who justify the wicked for a bribe, and take away the rights of the ones who are in the right!

Bribery causes the wicked to be declared just and the righteous unjust. There is an unspoken word, if you have enough money you can do anything with impurity. Further, it is common knowledge for the right amount of money you can obtain what rightfully belongs to another. Pick up a newspaper any day of the week to see this in black and white.

> *Amos 5:12, For I know your transgressions are many and your sins are great, You who distress the righteous and accept bribes and turn aside the poor in the gate.*

It is a shame when a poor man cannot get justice because he does not have the money to pay a bribe. When we lived in Kenya the news was filled with stories about the wealthy and mighty of the country not being prosecuted for crimes because bribes were paid. With enough money you have your court case dismissed because the file would disappear. Justice was determined by the amount of money you had.

> *Micah 3:11, Her leaders pronounce judgment for a bribe, Her priests instruct for a price And her prophets divine for money. Yet they lean on the Lord saying, "Is not the Lord in our midst? Calamity will not come upon us."*

The prophet Micah describes a nation about to come under the judgment of God. Bribery is one of the causes of this coming judgement. When a nation has reached a point where bribery is part and parcel of everyday life, even in the church, beware of the judgment of God.

> *Luke 22:4 – 5, And he went away and discussed with the chief priests and officers how he might betray Him to them. They were glad and agreed to give him money.*

Judas betrayed the Lord Jesus Christ because of the bribes of the priests. We are told Judas kept the money bag and always had his hand in it. It seems he would do anything for money. Would you?

Acts 8:18 – 21, Now when Simon saw that the Spirit was bestowed through the laying on of the apostles' hands, he offered them money, saying, "Give this authority to me as well, so that everyone on whom I lay my hands may receive the Holy Spirit." But Peter said to him, "May your silver perish with you, because you thought you could obtain the gift of God with money! You have no part or portion in this matter, for your heart is not right before God.

Simon offered the Apostles a bribe to give him the power to lay hands on people to receive the Baptism in the Holy Spirit. This revealed the condition of his heart. He was not interested in the power of the Holy Spirit to be a witness. He wanted to be an important person and make some money. There are men in the ministry today with the same motives and attitude Simon had. They stand the chance of perishing with their money.

Acts 24:26, At the same time too, he was hoping that money would be given him by Paul; therefore he also used to send for him quite often and converse with him.

Governor Felix wanted Paul to give him a bribe to release Paul from prison. For two years Paul was held in prison. Many times he was called before Felix and given the opportunity to offer a bribe for his release. Paul could have rationalized giving the bribe because of the teaching and preaching he could do if released from prison. Think of the people who could have been saved and the churches planted if Paul had paid the bribe for his release. Paul would rather stay in prison than break the laws of God for his release because he knew God would not bless his ministry if he won his release by bribery. The end does not justify the means.

The Bible has much to say on the subject of bribery. Everything referenced in the Word of God about bribery is negative. Nowhere does the Bible condone bribery. It is part of our everyday lives. The body of Christ must take a stand against bribery at all cost. To see bribery stopped in our nations we must be willing to pay the price to stand up and say bribery is sin; it must stop. It may take longer for us to get things done (for example of the permit mentioned earlier) or some project may never get approved without bribery. It is ok because God is looking at our hearts, not at the amount of money we get. It is much better in the eyes of God to accomplish a little with honesty, that great things through bribery.

Two Examples

One of our friends was working as the manager of a large farm at the Kenyan coast. He discovered his boss was doing things illegally by paying bribes for government officials to look the other way. When he discovered this he approached his boss about it, saying the bribery must stop or he could no longer work for him. As a result he lost his job. There was a young evangelist who was in a taxi on the way to a crusade he was holding. When the taxi was stopped at a road block this evangelist saw the driver give the policeman a bribe. The evangelist jumped out of the taxi and told the policeman what he was doing was wrong. The driver unloaded the evangelist's entire luggage and the taxi left him arguing with the policeman. After a few minutes a large Volvo pulled up with the area MP (Member of Parliament) inside. The MP got out of the car to ask what the problem was. When he was told the story he took the policeman's badge number and told the evangelist to come with him. The MP drove the young evangelist all the way to the venue for the crusade. The evangelist was willing to miss his meeting to stand up for righteousness and God supernaturally delivered him to his meeting.

Take a stand for righteousness and walk in integrity. If we will stand up for what is right, then God will stand up for us. The truth stands, "with God on your side who can defeat you?"

Assignment

- Record in your journal the fresh insights God gives you as you meditate on this lesson.
- Give examples of times you have been confronted with this blockade.
- How did you respond at that time?

- How would you respond now as a result of this lesson?
- Do you feel this is an issue in the church today?
- How can this impact this church?

Lesson Two – Dishonesty

Dishonesty means doing things which are illegal, immoral or unscriptural. It includes all types of lying, cheating, fraud, deception, and other practices which are not honest. If something is legal according to government but is illegal according to the Word of God we must obey the Word. Do not fall into the trap of doing dishonest things to gain wealth. Even if we become abundantly rich by dishonest means we will pay the penalty in the end.

> *Deuteronomy 25:13 – 15, "You shall not have in your bag differing weights, a large and a small. You shall not have in your house differing measures, a large and a small. You shall have a full and just weight; you shall have a full and just measure, that your days may be prolonged in the land which the Lord your God gives you.*

> *Proverbs 11:1, A false balance is an abomination to the Lord, But a just weight is His delight.*

> *Proverbs 20:10, Differing weights and differing measures, both of them are abominable to the Lord.*

> *Proverbs 20:23, Differing weights are an abomination to the Lord, and a false scale is not good.*

If we are in business, all our business dealings must be honest. Our customers must be assured they are getting exactly what they are paying for. When we lived in the country of Haiti this was a constant battle. You could buy from the same person every day and every day you would have to watch to make sure your things were measured our properly. The common business practice in the market was to cheat the customer if possible. There are spiritual reasons Haiti is the poorest country in the Western Hemisphere; dishonesty costs!

Deuteronomy 27:17, 'Cursed is he who moves his neighbor's boundary mark.' And all the people shall say, 'Amen.'

Part of the law given in Deuteronomy dealt with property lines or boundaries. A person who would move the boundary marker on his neighbor's property was to come under a curse from God. We can see this dishonest means of gaining property in the land grabbing schemes today. This problem is faced by almost every nation in the world. The people who do these things today still come under the curse of God. I would rather have no land with God's blessings that millions of acres with God's curse.

> *Psalms 101:7, He who practices deceit shall not dwell within my house; He who speaks falsehood shall not maintain his position before me.*

Like bribery, dishonesty has Kingdom life consequences. Dishonesty will prevent us from fulfilling our God ordained destiny. It is better to be a doorkeeper in the house of God than to gain all the wealth of the world by dishonest means.

> *Proverbs 10:2, Ill-gotten gains do not profit, But righteousness delivers from death.*

> *Proverbs 13:11, Wealth obtained by fraud dwindles, But the one who gathers by labor increases it.*

> *Proverbs 20:17, Bread obtained by falsehood is sweet to a man, But afterward his mouth will be filled with gravel.*

> *Proverbs 21:6, The acquisition of treasures by a lying tongue is a fleeting vapor, the pursuit of death.*

> *Proverbs 28:6, Better is the poor who walks in his integrity than he who is [a]crooked though he be rich.*

One of the injustices in the world is when people do get rich through dishonest means. Look at the wealth of drug dealers or mafia bosses. True they have a lot of money, but they also live in fear for their lives. The Bible says, riches gained by dishonest means only last for the present. True riches and true wealth are stored in heaven and will last for eternity. A person can be buried in a solid gold casket filled with money, but it will do him no good. Solomon said he would rather be poor with integrity than to be rich by dishonest means. (Whether he followed his own advice is another story.)

> *Habakkuk 2:9 – 9, Woe to him who gets evil gain for his house to put his nest on high, to be delivered from the hand of calamity!*

> *Obadiah 4, "Though you build high like the eagle, though you set your nest among the stars, from there I will bring you down," declares the Lord.*

The prophet Habakkuk warned the people of Israel about dishonest gain. It seems there were people in Israel who would do anything for money. They wanted to be great people. They wanted to be the big man of their area. Their dishonest gain allowed them to set themselves above other people. Because of their wealth the people looked up to them. The prophet cries "Woe" to such people. Obadiah says the Lord brings such people down.

In the New Testament, dishonesty brought judgement upon God's people. The disciples were selling all they had and giving the money to the Apostles to help meet the needs of the church (Acts 5:1 – 10). There was one couple, Ananias and Sapphira, who also sold their land. The only trouble was they were dishonest when they brought the money to the Apostles. They said, "Here is all the money we received from the sale of our property." The truth was it was only part of the money. God's judgment fell and both of them died at the feet of the Apostles. Their sin was not holding back part of the money, which was their right to do. It was being dishonest about it. They wanted to be known as great givers; people who gave all to God. Peter said they had not only been dishonest before men but also before God. What would happen today if God struck down everyone who was dishonest in the church?

> *Romans 13:6-7, For because of this you also pay taxes, for rulers are servants of God, devoting themselves to this very thing. 7 Render to all what is due them: tax to whom tax is*

due; custom to whom custom; fear to whom fear; honor to whom honor.

Paul taught the Roman Church to honor and obey the government authorities placed over them. He said these people were God's ministers to care for people. The Romans were admonished to pay their taxes and all other fees due to the government. Remember, the Roman government was one of the most godless governments in history, yet Paul told them to obey the government and pay their taxes. We must take this teaching to heart. There are many of God's people who are dishonest in the area of taxes. They go to a shop to purchase an item they need without getting a receipt to avoid paying taxes. Or they rationalize, why should I pay taxes when nothing is being done with the money to benefit me? Maybe they do not list cash payments in their ledger so they do not have to pay as much income tax. All of these are dishonest behaviors, which may block the flow of God's blessings in our lives.

> *2 Corinthians 4:1 -2, Therefore, since we have this ministry, as we received mercy, we do not lose heart, but we have renounced the things hidden because of shame, not walking in craftiness or adulterating the word of God, but by the manifestation of truth commending ourselves to every man's conscience in the sight of God.*

Another area where some Christians fall into dishonesty is in their work. If we work for a company we are to honor the rules of that company. To take longer than we are given for a break is dishonest. It is stealing time from the company. To use company supplies for personal use is also stealing from the company. I know secretaries who write letters for the church on company time using company supplies and equipment. This is dishonest and is the same as stealing (unless you have verbal permission from your boss). Even so you should pay for all supplies being used.

After teaching this in one church the pastor got up and confessed before the congregation he had been having one of the sisters do the church letters at her job. He said when he got his own secretary with his own typewriter and supplies he would not want her to do other people's letters at his expense. He repented of what he had done and stopped the practice.

I have heard testimonies from believers, thanking God for receiving too much change from a purchase. That was not a blessing; it was a test to see if they were honest. The shopkeeper may not catch the mistake or ever know anything about it, but God does. If the shopkeeper had not given you enough change would you praise God because He had blessed the shop owner? No, you would storm back in the shop and demand he return what belongs to you. The attitude is, "I can keep what belongs to you (and it is a blessing from God) but you cannot keep what belongs to me." These kinds of actions demonstrate both immaturity and greed.

There was a Christian businessman flying from London to New York on British Airways. After arriving at his hotel in New York he discovered his wallet was missing. Inside the wallet was all of his credit cards and US $3000. The man called the BA ticket counter at the New York airport to report his missing wallet. He was told the plane had already departed New York going back to London. About a week later this man received a call from British Airways saying his wallet had been found. When he went to collect the wallet he was told a businessman had found the wallet and turned it into the airline. Everything was in the wallet, including the US $3000. This Christian businessman's first reaction was to thank God a Christian had not found the wallet. He thought if a Christian had found it they would have rejoiced and praised God for such a wonderful blessing. What a bad testimony for Christianity. We should be known as the most honest people in the world.

Thus, we must guard our lives against everything dishonest. Some of the things mentioned here may be so "normal" in your culture that you only now realize the offense. Allow the Holy Spirit to speak to you about these things. When something is shown to you, like the pastor who confessed, repented, and changed his actions, you can do the same. God is faithful and just to forgive us when we repent.

Assignment

- Record in your journal the fresh insight God gives you as you meditate on this lesson.
- Give examples of times you have been confronted with this blockade.
- How did you respond at the time?
- How would you respond now as a result of this lesson?
- Do you feel this is a big issue in the church today?
- How can this impact the church?

Lesson Three – Disobedience

Disobedience means not adhering to the laws of the government or the laws of God, or both. Sometimes we are disobedient out of ignorance of the law. That does not mean we will not suffer the penalty for the disobedience. I remember in Uganda I wanted to take a picture of the Jinja Dam. After stopping my car on top of the dam. I got out with my camera. Several police came running toward me yelling for me to stop. Even though I was ignorant of the fact that stopping on the dam was illegal, I had to go to the police station because of the offense. There are many Christians who are disobedient to God's Word, by not tithing or giving offerings. Even if this is done out of ignorance it is still disobedience.

As the children of God we must obey all the laws of government, except in cases where the law is against God's Word. In America abortion on demand is legal. Many Christians, who minister and lament, have gone to prison because of their protests against a law of the government which is against the Word of God. When we disobey the laws of the land to obey the Word of God we must be willing to pay the penalty. Daniel was thrown to the lions and three Hebrew children were put in the furnace.

We must obey God's Word and the leading of the Holy Spirit. If we do not obey the Bible it will be hard to obey the leading of God's Spirit.

> *1 Samuel 15:18 – 23, "and the Lord sent you on a mission, and said, 'Go and utterly destroy the sinners, the Amalekites, and fight against them until they are exterminated.' Why then did you not obey the voice of the Lord, but rushed upon the spoil and did what was evil in the sight of the Lord?" Then Saul said to Samuel, "I did obey the voice of the Lord, and went on the mission on which the Lord sent me, and have brought back Agag the king of Amalek, and have utterly destroyed the*

Amalekites. But the people took some of the spoil, sheep and oxen, the choicest of the things devoted to destruction, to sacrifice to the Lord your God at Gilgal." Samuel said, "Has the Lord as much delight in burnt offerings and sacrifices as in obeying the voice of the Lord? Behold, to obey is better than sacrifice, and to heed than the fat of rams. "For rebellion is as the sin of divination, and insubordination is as iniquity and idolatry. Because you have rejected the word of the Lord, He has also rejected you from being king."

Proverbs21:3, To do righteousness and justice is desired by the Lord more than sacrifice.

Isaiah 43:23 – 24, "You have not brought to Me the sheep of your burnt offerings, nor have you honored Me with your sacrifices, I have not burdened you with offerings, nor wearied you with incense. "You have bought Me not sweet cane with money, Nor have you filled Me with the fat of your sacrifices; Rather you have burdened Me with your sins, You have wearied Me with your iniquities.

One of the greatest examples of disobedience in the Bible, outside of Adam and Eve, was King Saul (1 Samuel 15). The prophet Samuel gave King Saul a sure word from God. God told Saul to completely destroy his enemy; he was to kill all the people and all the animals. After the victory, Saul kept King Agag alive and also took many of the animals. When he was confronted by Samuel about this he said he did not disobey. He said his motives were pure and he did what God told him to do. The animals were taken so they could worship God by offering Him sacrifices from the spoil of battle. Samuel told Saul God was going to take the Kingdom away from him because of his disobedience. It is better to obey than sacrifice (1 Samuel 15:22).

In our society today, people justify not paying taxes so they can have more money to put into work for God. They say they are being economical with God's money so it can be put to the best use. Yes,

God wants us to be good stewards of what He has given us and to make the best use of the money we have. However, He does not want this at the expense of our obedience. When we disobey we risk losing God's blessings in our lives; it is not worth the risk!

Jeremiah 22:21, "I spoke to you in your prosperity; but you said, 'I will not listen!' This has been your practice from your youth, that you have not obeyed My voice."

Genesis 3:8, They heard the sound of the Lord God walking in the garden in the cool of the day, and the man and his wife hid themselves from the presence of the Lord God among the trees of the garden.

Genesis 3:23-24, ...therefore the Lord God sent him out from the garden of Eden, to cultivate the ground from which he was taken. So He drove the man out; and at the east of the garden of Eden He stationed the cherubim and the flaming sword which turned every direction to guard the way to the tree of life.

Jesus said my sheep hear my voice (John 10:27)...but a runaway lamb is out of ear shot, so it is with a disobedient believer. We get to know the voice of God when we spend time in fellowship with Him. When we are disobedient we tend to shy away from the presence of the Father. Remember when you were a child and you disobeyed your father. It was not very pleasant to be around him so you tried to hide or avoid him. It is the same way when we disobey God. Adam and Eve hid themselves from the presence of God when they had disobeyed. Because of their disobedience they were driven from the presence of God. God did not leave them, in fact He came to them, clothed and protected them. Our disobedience does not drive God a way, we run for fear, giving God shame.

The sin of disobedience can have drastic effects on our lives. We have seen from the examples of Saul and Adam great losses suffered because of disobedience. Ask the Spirit of God to help you to be sensitive to the Word of God and to His voice. The people of God must be quick to obey when they hear the Word of God. Be doers of the Word and not hearers only. Be like the small child standing on a high wall who jumps into the arms of his father when the father says, "Jump, I will catch you." Let us be that trusting with God.

Assignment

- Record in your journal the fresh insights God gives you as you meditate on this lesson.
- Give examples of times you have been confronted with this blockade.
- How did you respond at the time?
- How would you respond now as a result of this lesson?
- Do you feel this is a big issue in the church today?
- How can this impact the church?

Lesson Four – Greed or Covetousness

Throughout the Bible the words greed and covetous are interchangeable. In the Old Testament the Hebrew word is <u>batsa</u>. It means to plunder, to finish, to pine after, to desire, and to long for. This word is translated both greed and covetous. The Greek word, in the New Testament is <u>pleonexia</u>. It means a desire to have more (always in a bad since) and is translated covetous. When you read through the Bible remember both greed and covetous have the same meaning.

The spirit of greed is one of the ruling spirits in many nations. You can see its grip on people from every strata of society. The church has not escaped the spirit of greed, which has infiltrated even the House of God. The spirit of greed causes people to seek material blessings at the expense of everything else. Greed will divide friends, families, businesses, and even churches. Greed shows a lack of trust in God. In the Name of Jesus we must stand against greed to rescue our friends, families, businesses, churches and nation.

> *Exodus 16:20, But they did not listen to Moses, and some left part of it until morning, and it bred worms and became foul; and Moses was angry with them.*

> *Numbers 11:31 – 34, Now there went forth a wind from the Lord and it brought quail from the sea, and let them fall beside the camp, about a day's journey on this side and a day's journey on the other side, all around the camp and about two cubits deep on the surface of the ground. The people spent all day and all night and all the next day, and gathered the quail (he who gathered least gathered ten homers) and they spread them out for themselves all around the camp. While the meat was still between their teeth, before it was chewed, the anger of the Lord was kindled against the people, and the Lord struck the people with a very severe plague. So the name of that place was*

called Kibroth-hattaavah, because there they buried the people who had been greedy.

The children of Israel, in spite of God's great deliverance, suffered from greed. God miraculously provided them with food in the desert in the form of manna. They were told to only collect what was needed for the day. The spirit of greed gripped some of them, so they gathered much more than was needed. As a result the extra bred worms and rotted quickly.

Another time the children of Israel wanted more than God was providing (a good definition of greed) so they complained to Moses. God, in His mercy, sent quail for them to eat as He had at the beginning. Again the spirit of greed took hold of them and they stayed up all day, all night, and all the next day gathering the quail. The least amount anybody gathered was over 60 bushels. As a result of their greed God sent a plague upon them.

> *2 Kings 5:25 – 27, But he went in and stood before his master. And Elisha said to him, "Where have you been, Gehazi?" And he said, "Your servant went nowhere." Then he said to him, "Did not my heart go with you, when the man turned from his chariot to meet you? Is it a time to receive money and to receive clothes and olive groves and vineyards and sheep and oxen and male and female servants? Therefore, the leprosy of Naaman shall cling to you and to your descendants forever." So he went out from his presence a leper as white as snow.*

When Naaman was healed of his leprosy he offered to pay Elisha for his services. Elisha told him he would take nothing from him because it was God who did the work. Naaman left Elisha and headed back home. Elisha's servant Gehazi had been listening to their conversation. The spirit of greed gripped him and he followed Naaman to receive something from him. Gehazi lied to Naaman and received gifts through deception. When he returned to Elisha he was confronted with his sin and the punishment was the leprosy of Naaman, passed on to his family forever.

Greed is a dangerous thing. It corrupts our morals and leads us to do things we would otherwise not do. When a person will do almost anything for money, it is a sign he is being influenced by a spirit of greed.

> *Psalms 10:3, For the wicked boasts of his heart's desire, and the greedy man curses and spurns the Lord.*

Wicked people bless the greedy and renounce the LORD. There is a principle here; people approve of people who are similar to themselves. Greed makes a person wicked and follows a wicked heart.

> *Proverbs 11:6, The righteousness of the upright will deliver them, but the treacherous will be caught by their own greed.*

Unfaithful people are controlled and driven by their lust (or greed) to have more. Some people act irrationally just to obtain a certain possession. Many become trapped by lust for power, compromising their belief in God and His Word to obtain what they need.

> *Proverbs 11:24, There is one who scatters, and yet increases all the more, and there is one who withholds what is justly due, and yet it results only in want.*

Greed leads to poverty, but a giving spirit will increase your wealth. It is a Biblical principle, if you give you will receive; but if you do not give you are not blessed. The world says, "Get all you can and hold onto all you get." This philosophy causes people to store up more money than they could use in several lifetimes. Even with all of that wealth they are not happy, because they do not know Jesus and are not working according to His Word. It has been said there are two dilemmas in the world, 1) Not getting what you desire and 2) Getting what you desire. Without Jesus both of these dilemmas will make you miserable. True happiness does not come from lots of money and possessions but from a relationship with Christ.

Proverbs 15:27, He who profits illicitly troubles his own house, but he who hates bribes will live.

The spirit of greed causes people to do things that potentially bring disaster to their families. Many people frequent casinos and racetracks because their greed drives them to gamble their money, hoping to get rich. There are thousands of homes that have been ruined because of this. This drug trade and other underworld activities can place a person's life and family in jeopardy.

Proverbs 23:21, For the heavy drinker and the glutton will come to poverty, and drowsiness will clothe one with rags.

Drunkenness and gluttony are simply two forms of greed, manifested in a very visual way. The constant desire for more can be a sign of a spirit of greed.

Proverbs 25:16, Have you found honey? Eat only what you need, that you not have it in excess and vomit it.

Take only what you need and can use. People have a tendency to take more than they need because they do not have the assurance that God can or will take care of them. This verse says if you take more than you need, you will find, it can cause unpleasant results.

Jeremiah 6:13, "For from the least of them even to the greatest of them, everyone is greedy for gain, and from the prophet even to the priest everyone deals falsely.

In the days of Jeremiah they had the same problem we see in many countries today. Greed had corrupted every aspect of society, even the temple. It is a sad day when even people who call themselves men of God are gripped with the spirit of greed. You hear of a minister who will not pray for people unless they are paid. If you want them to bless your home or your business you must pay them for their services. I know of some churches where you cannot advance in ministry without paying the person above you. It is time the people of God stood up and said enough is enough.

Luke 16:14, Now the Pharisees, who were lovers of money, were listening to all these things and were scoffing at Him.

Jesus warned the Pharisees about the love of money. These religious leaders were more concerned about their pockets than they were the things of God. Because of their love for money, they turned against and made fun of Jesus, the Messiah they had been longing for. Greed will blind our eyes to things most important. I have known ministries turning away from their God given calling because there was more money in other areas of ministry. Our call is not determined by the availability of funds but by what God reveals to us. If God has called us to a specific ministry then God will provide the resources needed to fulfill the vision.

Romans 1:28 – 32, And just as they did not see fit to acknowledge God any longer, God gave them over to a depraved mind, to do those things which are not proper, being filled with all unrighteousness, wickedness, greed, evil; full of envy, murder, strife, deceit, malice; they are gossips, slanderers, haters of God, insolent, arrogant, boastful, inventors of evil, disobedient to parents, without understanding, untrustworthy, unloving, unmerciful; and although they know the ordinance of God, that those who practice such things are worthy of death, they not only do the same, but also give hearty approval to those who practice them.

One of the signs a person is in danger with God is the spirit of greed. Over time people know what they are doing is wrong; they enjoy doing it! They even approve of others who do the same thing. I was talking to a man who told me he wanted to go to hell. He said he enjoyed the sin he was involved in so much he would rather go to hell than turn to God and stop what he was doing. What a sad condition to be in.

Ephesians 5:3, But immorality or any impurity or greed must not even be named among you, as is proper among saints;

As members of Christ, we are to live our lives without greed. The people of God should be known in the community as people who are givers, caring for the needs of others. When a brother or sister who has been overcome with the spirit of greed, we need to lovingly confront them and help them return in obedience to the Word of God.

1 Thessalonians 2:5, For we never came with flattering speech, as you know, nor with a pretext for greed—God is witness—

Paul was never greedy or covetous. He was concerned about getting the Word of God to as many peoples as possible. There were never grounds for accusing Paul of being in the ministry for money. When it was necessary he worked as a tent maker to support his work. He was even supportive of other ministries saying that all worked for God and only God could cause true growth.

1 Timothy 6:10, For the love of money is a root of all sorts of evil, and some by longing for it have wandered away from the faith and pierced themselves with many griefs.

I have heard many preachers proclaim that money is the root of all evil. That is not what the scripture declares. It is not money itself, but the love, or lust for money that creates evil. Money in and of itself is amoral, neither good nor bad. The problem comes when people love money more than they love God. The love of money will cause a person to do anything for it, hoping that greater possessions will provide a better quality of life. It is the love of money that causes Christians to compromise their beliefs in order to possess more position, prestige or power through money. If a person does not see their sin and repent of this greed they will stray from the faith and it will cause them a world of trouble.

2 Peter 2:2-3, Many will follow their sensuality, and because of them the way of the truth will be maligned; and in their greed they will exploit you with false words; their judgment from long ago is not idle, and their destruction is not asleep.

I know of good Christians who have lost money in business deals with other Christians who were filled with greed. One man tells of how he invested in a gold mine which was being promoted by a well-known and well respected Christian business man. This business man knew the gold mine was not real, but he took people's money anyway. The businessman left the country and the people lost their entire fortunes.

Before you invest in any project or scheme, you need to pray and get the mind of God. Anyone can be fooled...but God help the perpetrator of this kind of deception.

Assignment:

- Record in your journal the fresh insights God gives you as you meditate on this lesson.
- Give examples of times you have been confronted with the issue of Greed.
- How did you respond?
- How might you respond differently now that you have studied this lesson?
- Do you feel that greed is a real problem in the church today?
- What impact has or does greed have on the church and the expansion of God's Kingdom?

Lesson Five - Laziness

Laziness or slothfulness (some translations say sluggard) is seen in a person willing to do only what is needed to get by. They do not work or perform up to their best potential. Laziness is a bad witness for Christ. I have heard employers say they would rather not hire a Christian because they were poor workers. Believers should be the best and hardest working people there are because we are not working for our employer but for God. Laziness not only deals with work but with every area of our lives.

> *Proverbs 6:6-11, Go to the ant, O sluggard, Observe her ways and be wise, Which, having no chief Officer or ruler, Prepares her food in the summer and gathers her provision in the harvest. How long will you lie down, O sluggard? When will you arise from your sleep? "A little sleep, a little slumber, a little folding of the hands to rest"— Your poverty will come in like a vagabond and your need like an armed man.*

Man can learn many things from God's creation. In this passage King Solomon tells the lazy person he should watch the ants' behavior. By simple observation, one can see that survival only comes from diligent work. There is no leader commanding the ant to work yet the ant, by nature, works to gather food for the winter. Solomon also warns poverty will come upon a lazy man like a robber. The robber strikes without warning and when you least expect it. If you are lazy, be warned. One day poverty will overtake you and you will have nothing. Be watchful so you can learn from those around you.

> *Proverbs 10:4, Poor is he who works with a negligent hand, but the hand of the diligent makes rich.*

Laziness and poverty are closely related and where you find the one you will normally find the other. On the other hand, a lifestyle of diligence will bring a person wealth. We have a choice to make. Will we live in poverty or wealth? It depends on our work ethic. If we are lazy we choose poverty; if we are diligent we choose wealth.

Proverbs 13:4, The soul of the sluggard craves and gets nothing, but the soul of the diligent is made fat.

The soul or thinking of a person determines what he or she does. Our desires are only realized by hard work. The desires of the diligent will be fulfilled because by his hard work he will earn the means to see them fulfilled. If we have unfulfilled desires it is probably because we are not doing all we could or should be doing. We must honestly assess our hearts to ensure we are doing our part.

Proverbs 14:4, Where no oxen are, the manger is clean, but much revenue comes by the strength of the ox.

This is a very vivid picture Solomon presents us. We can have a clean barn if we do not have any oxen. But without oxen (the right tools) no work gets done. If we want to use the oxen to do the work we will also have to be willing to clean up the mess. There is work involved in maintaining the things we use in our work. The bottom line is - only hard work will bring wealth and blessings to us.

Proverbs 18:9, He also who is slack in his work is brother to him who destroys.

When we are not diligent in our work we allow destruction to occur. If you look at the infrastructure of many nations you will see this principle at work. The reason roads are so bad is because of the negligence of the highway department. If they had been diligent to repair the roads when they first needed repair they would not have been destroyed. This is one example of many.

Proverbs 19:15, Laziness casts into a deep sleep, and an idle man will suffer hunger.

Lazy people lie around doing little or nothing, and then they wonder why they are hungry. If we do not want to suffer hunger we must be diligent to work as hard as we can. I have known people who will sleep the whole day and then go out and beg for food. If they are offered work they will refuse, expecting people to give them food. They are suffering because of their own laziness.

Proverbs 20:4, The person who does not work will end up begging. He finds excuses for his lack of productivity. His lack of preparation for work will mean he will have little or nothing to reap on payday. As a result he will complain about his lot in life, and end up begging for food. If we want to have a good harvest we must be diligent to work hard during the planting season. If there is no sowing there can be no reaping.

Proverbs 20:13, The sluggard does not plow after the autumn, so he begs during the harvest and has nothing.

A person cannot do work if he always loves to sleep. Those who get up early to go to work will be satisfied with food.

Proverbs 21:25-26, The desire of the sluggard puts him to death, for his hands refuse to work; all day long he is craving, while the righteous gives and does not hold back.

In 1992 a group of Kenyan's were starving because of famine. When a truck load of food was taken to their village they refused to help unload the food. Their attitude was, "If the government is sending the food to us let the government send someone to unload it for us." The man driving the truck left the village and took the entire load back to the warehouse. Many of those people died because their hands refused to work. They allowed their pride to keep them from working which resulted in the deaths of many people.

Proverbs 24:20-34, For there will be no future for the evil man; The lamp of the wicked will be put out. My son, fear the Lord and the king; Do not associate with those who are given to change, For their calamity will rise suddenly, and who knows the ruin that comes from both of them? These also are sayings of the wise. To show partiality in judgment is not good. He who says to the wicked, "You are righteous." Peoples will curse him, nations will abhor him; But to those who rebuke the wicked will be delight, and a good blessing will come upon them. He kisses the lips who gives a right answer .Prepare your work outside and make it ready for yourself in the field; Afterwards, then, build your house. Do not be a witness against your neighbor without cause, and do not deceive with your lips. Do not say, "Thus I shall do to him as he has done to me; I will render to the man according to his work." I passed by the field of the sluggard and by the vineyard of the man lacking sense, and behold, it was completely overgrown with thistles; Its surface was covered with nettles and its stone wall was broken down. When I saw, I reflected upon it; I looked, and received instruction. "A little sleep, a little slumber, a little folding of the hands to rest," Then your poverty will come as a robber and your want like an armed man.

The field and the vineyard did not become over grown over night. This happened gradually over a long period of time. The trap of laziness comes from a belief that one can be lazy for a season and still prosper. The vineyard and the field will continue to give fruit for a season, but will eventually, and sooner than later, run out. To have a maximum harvest we must be diligent all the time and never allow the weeds to take root. Prosperity comes from consistent, long term work.

2 Thessalonians 3:7-12, For you yourselves know how you ought to follow our example, because we did not act in an undisciplined manner among you, nor did we eat anyone's bread without paying for it, but with labor and hardship we kept working night and day so that we would not be a burden to any of you; not because we do not have the right to this, but in order to offer ourselves as a model for you, so that you would follow our example. For even when we were with you, we used to give you this order: if anyone is not willing to work, then he is not to eat, either. For we hear that some among you are leading an undisciplined life, doing no work at all, but acting like busybodies. Now such persons we command and exhort in the Lord Jesus Christ to work in quiet fashion and eat their own bread.

The Apostle Paul worked with his hands to support his ministry so he would not be accused of being a burden to the people. Paul also taught that those who preach the gospel should live by the gospel. There is no shame in a man of God working a secular job to support his ministry and his family if the ministry is not able to support him. On the other hand there is nothing wrong with a man being supported fully by the ministry as long as he is putting in a full day's work for a full day's pay. The problem comes when a man of God receives support from the ministry but does not work as hard as he should.

Paul also makes the statement if a man does not work neither should he eat. If you have a relative who comes to live with you and refuses to work you should not feed them. This does not mean they have to have a job. There are many things around the house they can do. The dishes must be washed after every meal. Maybe there is a need for someone to watch the children while you are at work. Does the grass need to be cut? If they refuse to work there should be no plate on the table for them. Do not say but that is not allowed in our culture, we must take care of those who come to us. We are not talking about culture, we are talking about being obedient to the word of God. If we allow someone a free ride we facilitate their downward spiral towards poverty. By standing up for the scriptures you are helping them to get off the road to poverty and on the road to success.

Assignment

- Record in your journal the fresh insights God gives you as you meditate on this lesson.
- Are there times when you have allowed yourself to be lazy? What was the result?

- How did you respond at the time?
- How would you respond now as a result of this lesson?
- Do you feel this is a problem in the church today?
- How can this impact your church?

Lesson Six - Pride

Pride is the root from which many sins originate. If one would trace many of the things we do to their root cause we would find the ugly sin of pride. The sin of pride is what caused the devil to be chased from heaven. He said he wanted to be like God and even to be above God. The sin of pride causes us to always want to look good, important and powerful before others. Pride will keep us from admitting when we are wrong. In the New Testament the word translated pride, proud, haughty, high-minded, and others is tuphoo. This word means to be wrapped in smoke. That is a good definition of pride. Pride means to be so wrapped up in the smoke screen of our own importance people cannot see what we really are. The Old Testament word is gaavah which means arrogance, pomp, swelling, haughtiness, and highness. Pride causes people to inflate themselves to be better than others. The sin of pride will cause the blessings of God to be blocked in our lives.

> *Deuteronomy 8:13-14, 17, 19, ... and when your herds and your flocks multiply, and your silver and gold multiply, and all that you have multiplies, then your heart will become proud and you will forget the Lord your God who brought you out from the land of Egypt, out of the house of slavery....Otherwise, you may say in your heart, 'My power and the strength of my hand made me this wealth.'...It shall come about if you ever forget the Lord your God and go after other gods and serve them and worship them, I testify against you today that you will surely perish.*

Be careful not to attribute the blessings of God to your own abilities. He does not share His glory with anyone*. Everything we have has come from God. We should always give God the glory for His blessings. There are people who trust in their jobs to meet their needs, not putting their trust in God at all times. In reality, it is God who gives them the ability to work so they need to acknowledge His hand at work at all times. In other words, gratitude for God's blessings, acknowledging him as our source defeats pride.

Psalms 10:1-4, Why do You stand afar off, O LORD? Why do You hide *Yourself* in times of trouble? In pride the wicked hotly pursue the afflicted; Let them be caught in the plots which they have devised. For the wicked boasts of his heart's desire, and the greedy man curses *and* spurns the LORD. The wicked, in the haughtiness of his countenance, does not seek *Him.* All his thoughts are, "There is no God."

If we want to stand alone, a self-made man, God will leave us alone. Pride leads the wicked to persecute the poor rather than seek God. A person who is lifted up in pride does not acknowledge God in his life.

> *Psalms 30:6, Now as for me, I said in my prosperity, "I will never be moved."*

- Of note is John 17, where Jesus' desire is to share his glory with his disciples'. They had sacrificed their lives for the mission, and Jesus heart was to share with his comrades the very glory of God.

King David said he was completely secure because of his great prosperity. It was not many years later David was on the run from his son Absalom.

It is said that hundreds of successful and wealthy men took their own lives when the stock market went bust in 1929. They determined it was better to be dead than poor, having put their trust in their riches. David looked at his great wealth and position as King and thought there was nothing he could not accomplish. For a season he forgot where he came from. He was who he was because of the favor of God. He soon learned when God lifts His hand we can quickly lose all we thought we had accomplished. While David was running in the wilderness, living in caves, his great wealth and position was not able to help him. He learned he could only rely upon the Lord as his source.

Psalms 59:12, On account of the sin of their mouth and the words of their lips, Let them even be caught in their pride, and on account of curses and lies which they utter.

Words spoken in pride will eventually come back to bite us. Prideful boasting will take us captive because it refuses to acknowledge God. We must guard our mouth so as not to speak things out of pride. Speaking the truth in humility is the only sure way to avoid prideful boasting. Be sure to always give God the glory for what he has done.

Proverbs 8:13, "The fear of the Lord is to hate evil; Pride and arrogance and the evil way and the perverted mouth, I hate.

When the fear of the Lord is ruling our lives we will hate the same things the Lord hates. Notice how many scriptures we have shared in this section that link pride and the mouth together. Many times our pride is expressed by the words of our mouth.

Proverbs 11:2, When pride comes, then comes dishonor, but with the humble is wisdom.

Pride brings shame but humility brings wisdom. When a person is speaking out of pride they are usually devoid of wisdom, they are trying to make themselves look better than they really are. Humility does not try to build the speaker up but builds God up.

Proverbs 13:10, Through insolence comes nothing but strife, but wisdom is with those who receive counsel.

Much of the contention and fighting in our churches is a result of pride. People want to be the leader or they want to have power in church. They are not interested in the well-being of the church but in getting what they want. The person who receives wise counsel has the best interest of the church at heart and will speak in wisdom. We should be more concerned for the welfare of the church than we are for our own ego.

Proverbs 15:25, The Lord will tear down the house of the proud, but He will establish the boundary of the widow.

Pride is simply putting ourselves before the Lord. Because the Lord loves us, he will do whatever is necessary to break our pride. In this passage when it says the house of the proud it is speaking about the person's way of life. If we allow pride to build up in our heart we will stop the flow of God's blessings in our lives. Solomon contrasts the proud with the widow. Widows were looked upon as the most humble of people. Humility means we put God first, others second and ourselves last. We show our humility by lifting others up, not by putting ourselves down. We make the choice whether to be proud or humble. Choose wisely.

Proverbs 16:18, Pride goes before destruction, and a haughty spirit before stumbling.

One of the first signs a man is on the road to destruction is pride. Pride is the beginning of the fall of any man. When we allow pride to rule our lives we turn our backs on God, setting ourselves up as lord of our lives. The truth is, we do not have the wisdom and knowledge to run our lives. It is only when we take self off of the throne of our lives and allow Jesus his rightful place that we experience the full blessings of God. Choose the way of pride and it will lead you straight to destruction.

Proverbs 18:23, The poor man utters supplications, but the rich man answers roughly.

The rich man says in his heart, "It does not matter how I treat others because they are only after my money." That attitude turns people's hearts to stone. God can only bless us when we are filled with compassion. Many a man has been trapped by the devil because of the harsh words he has spoken to the poor. The Bible cautions us to place a guard on our lips.

Proverbs 28:11, The rich man is wise in his own eyes, but the poor who has understanding sees through him.

It is funny how some people think. They assume because they have lots of money they know everything. They will try to give advice on every subject and never ask for the advice of others. In his own estimate he is wise even when everyone else knows he is not. Even a poor man with wisdom can see through the shallow logic of these people. All the money in the world can never buy the wisdom of God. There is nothing wrong with being rich as long as you do not allow your riches to make you proud. There are many rich people who are humble just like there are many poor who are proud. It is a matter of the heart, not a matter of money.

Proverbs 29:23, A man's pride will bring him low, but a humble spirit will obtain honor.

Pride puffs up a person's ego. It makes people think more of themselves than they should. Pride will bring a man low and only humility will bring honor to a person. You may ask how this scripture relates to a teaching on finances. If a person becomes proud because of their riches, pride will bring them down. Pride in riches may be the thing that leads to a reversal in financial standing. Do not get me wrong here; there is nothing wrong with being wealthy as long as we continue to be humble before God and man. The only time we get into trouble is when we allow pride to come in because of our riches.

Jeremiah 9:23, Thus says the Lord, "Let not a wise man boast of his wisdom, and let not the mighty man boast of his might, let not a rich man boast of his riches;

Remember, everything we have comes from God. The prophet mentions several things we are not to be proud of: wisdom, strength, and riches. He goes on to say we should be proud we know God and understand that God exercises loving kindness, judgment, and righteousness in the earth. I have known people who trusted in and boasted about their intellectual achievements. They believed they were too smart to need God. Pride in their wisdom was a blockade to them accepting Jesus and receiving His blessings.

> *Ezekiel 28:4 – 7, "By your wisdom and understanding you have acquired riches for yourself and have acquired gold and silver for your treasuries. "By your great wisdom, by your trade you have increased your riches and your heart is lifted up because of your riches— Therefore thus says the Lord God, because you have made your heart like the heart of God, Therefore, behold, I will bring strangers upon you, the most ruthless of the nations. And they will draw their swords against the beauty of your wisdom and defile your splendor.*

If your heart is lifted up because of your riches beware. These people took all the credit for their great accomplishments. They did not realize it was God who gave them the wisdom and understanding to be successful in their business ventures. It was because of pride God allows their destruction. God does not judge them because of their wealth or success, but because they do not acknowledge him or give him the glory for their success.

> *1 Timothy 6:3-6, If anyone advocates a different doctrine and does not agree with sound words, those of our Lord Jesus Christ, and with the doctrine conforming to godliness, he is conceited and understands nothing; but he has a morbid interest in controversial questions and disputes about words, out of which arise envy, strife, abusive language, evil suspicions, and constant friction between men of depraved mind and deprived of the truth, who suppose that godliness is a means of gain. But godliness actually is a means of great gain when accompanied by contentment.*

Thus far we have concentrated on people who are proud of their wealth or wisdom. The Apostle Paul states people can be proud of the things of God. False teachers are proud of the things they teach, but in reality they teach to gain followers and honorariums. They bring upon themselves envy, strife, reviling, suspicions, and ungodliness. We are warned to stay away from people like this.

Paul states great gain comes from true godliness with contentment. A person is truly rich when he is content with what he has.

> *1 Timothy 6:17, Instruct those who are rich in this present world not to be conceited or to fix their hope on the uncertainty of riches, but on God, who richly supplies us with all things to enjoy.*

Timothy was the leader of the church in Ephesus, a city of renown, with many wealthy people living there. Undoubtedly, there were some wealthy men and women who had come to faith, and were a part of local congregations. Paul reminds Timothy of what is most important. All riches in this life are a blessing from God, but does not mean one is more spiritual, more loved by God, is special in other ways. When God makes us rich, there is not sorrow added to it…we must learn to be grateful and generous, for the reason for our wealth is to be a blessing to others.

> *2 Timothy 3:1 – 7, But realize this, that in the last days difficult times will come. For men will be lovers of self, lovers of money, boastful, arrogant, revilers, disobedient to parents, ungrateful, unholy, unloving, irreconcilable, malicious gossips, without self-control, brutal, haters of good, treacherous, reckless, conceited, lovers of pleasure rather than lovers of God, holding to a form of godliness, although they have denied its power; Avoid such men as these. For among them are those who enter into households and captivate weak women weighed down with sins, led on by various impulses, always learning and never able to come to the knowledge of the truth.*

Pride is one of the sins prevalent today. Look around you and you will see people who are dripping with pride. It can be seen in athletes, actors, businessmen, politicians, average citizens and even Christians. When we look at the signs of the times we know we are living in perilous days.

Revelation 3:17 – 18, Because you say, "I am rich, and have become wealthy, and have need of nothing," and you do not know that you are wretched and miserable and poor and blind and naked, I advise you to buy from Me gold refined by fire so that you may become rich, and white garments so that you may clothe yourself, and that the shame of your nakedness will not be revealed; and eye salve to anoint your eyes so that you may see.

We need to see ourselves the way God sees us. Our wealth and security are nothing in the eyes of God. We need to pray for God to open our eyes that we may see our true condition without Him. Outside of Jesus we are nothing. We are truly something and somebody when we are in Christ.

Assignment

- Record in your journal the fresh insights God gives you as you meditate on this lesson.
- Give examples of times you have struggled with pride.
- How did you respond at the time?
- How would you respond now as a result of this lesson?
- Do you see pride as a major problem in churches today? Amongst leaders? Give examples.
- How can this impact the church?

Lesson Seven - Respect of Persons

James 2:1 – 3, My brethren, do not hold your faith in our glorious Lord Jesus Christ with an attitude of personal favoritism. For if a man comes into your assembly with a gold ring and dressed in fine clothes, and there also comes in a poor man in dirty clothes, and you pay special attention to the one who is wearing the fine clothes, and say, "You sit here in a good place," and you say to the poor man, "You stand over there, or sit down by my footstool,"

James 2:9, But if you show partiality, you are committing sin and are convicted by the law as transgressors.

There are exceptions to the every rule, but by and large, the principle is true that it is your common man and woman that supports the work of the ministry, not major benefactors. Again, there are exceptions, and they are usually exceptional ones…such as Abraham, David in providing for the building of the Temple in Jerusalem, the women that supported Jesus' ministry and Barnabas, who sold a piece of land and gave the money to the apostles. But again, these major benefactors are rarer than one might think and the best of them simply know that this is their gift, the gift of giving, and they expect no strings or special benefits for their giving.

If someone was to give our ministry a large gift, we would be grateful, and would certainly give acknowledgement for their gift…but that would not mean they would be given the best seats in the house, or special access to leadership. Everyone in and outside of the Body of Christ deserves respect. But to show preference to someone, a politician, a pastor, or anyone else over the "common sinner" is wrong, and to be avoided.

Assignment

- Record in your journal the fresh insights God gives you as you meditate on this lesson.
- Have you encountered partiality in the church? When, how, and what was your reaction to it?
- Do you feel this is a big issue in the church today?
- How can this impact this church?

Lesson Eight - Unforgiveness

Proverbs 28:13, He who conceals his transgressions will not prosper, but he who confesses and forsakes them will find compassion.

One of the keys to our prosperity is a heart of repentance. As long as people cover their sin they will never prosper financially or in the things of God. Unforgiveness blocks the blessings of God from flowing in our lives. On the other hand, if we are quick to confess our sin, repent and ask for the Lord's forgiveness we will be shown mercy. Those who are covered with the mercy of God will prosper in everything they do.

Matthew 6:14-15, For if you forgive others for their transgressions, your heavenly Father will also forgive you. But if you do not forgive others, then your Father will not forgive your transgressions.

One of the wonderful parts of our salvation is that our sins have been forgiven, past, present and future. Yet, in practical terms, forgiveness received needs to be forgiveness given...or consequences will naturally follow. If we forgive others God forgives us. If we do not forgive others God will not forgive us. When we say the Lord's Prayer we are asking God to forgive us just like we forgive other people. Our prayer should be for God to help us forgive people in the same way he forgives us. Our forgiving others is the key to receiving or fully experiencing the forgiveness of God. It is a dangerous thing to hold unforgiveness in our hearts, as it can lead to a root of bitterness that defiles us fully.

Mark 11:25-26, Whenever you stand praying, forgive, if you have anything against anyone, so that your Father who is in heaven will also forgive you your transgressions. [But if you do not forgive, neither will your Father who is in heaven forgive your transgressions."]

Before your prayers can be effective you must forgive others or God will not forgive you. Our prayers will not be heard as long as there is unforgiveness in our hearts. When you pray you must do so with a clean heart. If the Holy Spirit reveals to you there is something in your heart against another person be sure to forgive that person, so your prayer will be heard.

When I think about the spiritual blockades in our lives I am reminded of the drainage ditch outside of my home church in America. There is a very large ditch running through the property for the purpose of drainage during rains. This drainage ditch serves its purpose until a small branch flowing down the ditch gets caught across the pipe, which goes under the road. The small branch does not have much effect on the flow of this ditch. It simply serves as an anchor for other things to hold on to. After some time the water starts to back up because debris has caught on that small branch. If this debris is not cleared the entire ditch will become blocked. When this happens the water backs up, flooding the church property. The blockage started with one small branch.

It is the same way in our lives. When we allow one small sin in, others will gather and join with that sin until the entire flow of God's blessings cease. Daily we need to allow the Holy Spirit to inspect the flow of the river of blessing in our lives. When He finds something has blocked the flow we must allow Him to deal with it. Be quick to repent and clear out all the blockages in your heart.

Assignment

- Record in your journal the fresh insights God gives you as you meditate on this lesson.
- Give examples of times you have been confronted with this blockade.
- How did you respond at the time?
- How would you respond now as a result of this lesson?
- Do you feel this is an important issue in the church today?
- How can this impact this church?

Lesson Nine - Debt

Exodus 22:14, "If a man borrows anything from his neighbor, and it is injured or dies while its owner is not with it, he shall make full restitution.

When you borrow something, like a tool, and you break it, even accidentally, you need to replace it. We must be very careful about borrowing things, because it puts us under obligation to the owner to return what we borrow, in the same condition we received it.

Deuteronomy 28:12, The LORD will open for you His good storehouse, the heavens, to give rain to your land in its season and to bless all the work of your hand; and you shall lend to many nations, but you shall not borrow.

If possible, believers are not to borrow. It shows a lack of trust in God's provision. We are to believe the Word of God and stand upon His promises. God will supply as we put our full and complete trust in him.

Psalms 37:21, The wicked borrows and does not pay back, but the righteous is gracious and gives.

I have loaned many books to church members, never to see them again. Perhaps it was simply an oversight on their part. However, this scripture makes it clear, not to return something we borrow is wicked...so, I suppose there are a lot of wicked folks in the church!

Proverbs 3:27-28, Do not withhold good from those to whom it is due, when it is in your power to do it. Do not say to your neighbor, "Go, and come back, and tomorrow I will give it," when you have it with you.

When a debt is due and you have the money you are to repay the debt. Many people postpone payment as long as possible so they can use what has been borrowed as long as possible. If you need something for an extended period of time it is better to purchase the item than to borrow it. Borrowing leads to debt.

Proverbs 22:7, The rich rules over the poor, and the borrower becomes the lender's slave.

The consequences of borrowing are bondage (in some parts of the world, literal imprisonment). God does not want His people in bondage or servitude. Therefore, we must stay free of debt.

Habakkuk 2:6, "Will not all of these take up a taunt-song against him, even mockery and insinuations against him and say, 'Woe to him who increases what is not his—For how long—And makes himself rich with loans?'

One of the problems with developing nations is their debt load to developed nations. Their debt repayment places such a burden on the economy it is almost impossible to engage in meaningful development. Everything which comes in goes out as debt repayment. There are families who pay more to service debt than the money they earn each month. As a result they are always hounded by their creditors for payment. The consequences of debt can be devastating; do all you can to avoid it.

Romans 13:8, Owe nothing to anyone except to love one another; for he who loves his neighbor has fulfilled the law.

The only thing you should owe a person is love. God wants us to be love debtors to the whole world. This is a debt God Himself will help us pay. It is God's desire for His children to show his love to the world. We should be looking for opportunities to demonstrate the love of God.

Conclusion

Frankly, undisciplined spending, that is, the inability to live within ones means is a major problem in the church. Debt can crush the life out of individuals, place enormous stress on families, and damage the churches mission and message.

Assignment

- Record in your journal the fresh insights God gives you as you meditate on this lesson.
- If you have been but no longer are in debt, how did you get out of it?
- If you are in debt, and know you needed to deal with it, what is your plan to do so? Do you have someone to help you? (a planner, a pastor, not a Westerner to pay off your bills!)
- Do you feel this is a major issue in the church today?
- How can the problem of debt impact the church?

Lesson Ten - Hastening to Get Rich

Proverbs 10:22, It is the blessing of the Lord that makes rich, and He adds no sorrow to it.

God's desire is for His people to trust Him to meet all their needs. When God blesses His people there is no sorrow, only blessing. God wants His children to be blessed and content in him.

Proverbs 21:5, The plans of the diligent lead surely to advantage, but everyone who is hasty comes surely to poverty.

Anything worth doing requires faithful, diligent effort. Simply stated, diligence is rewarded with plenty. On the other hand, those who are always looking for the easy money end up in poverty. If something seems to be too good to be true, it probably is too good to be true.

Proverbs 23:4-5, Do not weary yourself to gain wealth, cease from your consideration of it. When you set your eyes on it, it is gone. For wealth certainly makes itself wings like an eagle that flies toward the heavens.

This scripture speaks to the person who spends all their time in the pursuit of money. God is jealous for his children, and wants his children to spend time with him. When we neglect our relationship with God in the pursuit of riches God, will allow riches to elude us as a bird who flies away.

Proverbs 24:3-4, By wisdom a house is built, and by understanding it is established; And by knowledge the rooms are filled with all precious and pleasant riches.

Wisdom and knowledge are gained by hard work. Our pursuit first must be for God, then for wisdom, understanding and lastly for knowledge. It is not the pursuit of riches which gives life meaning, but Godly wisdom and understanding.

> *Proverbs 28:19-22, He who tills his land will have plenty of food, but he who follows empty pursuits will have poverty in plenty. A faithful man will abound with blessings, but he who makes haste to be rich will not go unpunished. To show partiality is not good, because for a piece of bread a man will transgress. A man with an evil eye hastens after wealth and does not know that want will come upon him.*

Any worker who is diligent to work hard will have plenty to eat. Those who follow after frivolous pursuits for money will end up in poverty. Sometimes people do "luck out" and "fall into" riches. However, most men and women who are constantly pursuing wealth have nothing to show for it, because the pursuit of wealth is, "easy come, and easy go."

> *Proverbs 31:16, 24, She considers a field and buys it; from her earnings she plants a vineyard. ...She makes linen garments and sells them, and supplies belts to the tradesmen*

Most successful businesses are built on sound financial planning and business strategy. This is true for churches as well. We see here the virtuous woman was diligent in her planning and she was blessed. There is the old saying, "fail to plan and you plan to fail."

> *1 Timothy 6:9, But those who want to get rich fall into temptation and a snare and many foolish and harmful desires which plunge men into ruin and destruction.*

Desiring to be rich brings many temptations and snares. In our town we have several casinos. These gambling establishments are filled with people who want to make quick money. They have thrown reason out the window, spending their hard earned money trying to defeat the odds and hit the jackpot. The only ones getting rich in the casinos are the owners. Some people will do anything if they think they can make some quick money. Internet scams only work because they cater to people's desire to get rich quick.

Assignment

- Record in your journal the fresh insights God gives you as you meditate on this lesson.
- Give examples of times you have been confronted with this problem.
- Do you feel this is a big issue in the church today?
- How can this impact this church?

Lesson Eleven - Impulse Spending

Impulse spending is a major cause of debt and distress in families. It is defined as buying something you really do not need just because you see it and want it. Sadly, we have seen many believers collect their pay and head straight for the shopping center, so they can buy something they "just cannot live without"! Once they have money in their pocket they spend with little thought for the larger needs of their family, only later to realize they no longer have the money to pay bills and eat.

Be careful when you shop. Store owners spend thousands of dollars on marketing research designed to get you into their stores. One way to avoid impulse buying is to shop with a list and only buy the things on the list which you clearly need. Do not shop just to kill time. You may end up killing your finances.

Further, avoid buying something on looks alone. That got Eve into a lot of trouble. Genesis 3:6 says the fruit was pleasant to the eyes. Her attention was first fixated on the beauty of the fruit, then she later fell for the "sales pitch". Stores know how to make things look very appealing, often better than they really are.

Here are a few things merchants use to get you to buy now.

- On Sale - Best price in town
- Last item in stock - buy now
- Enjoy it now - pay later
- Going out of business sale

When I (Dr. Steve) first visited Kenya in 1984, there was a store in Nairobi which had a sign in the window "going out of business ever thing 50% off." The sign stayed in the window for more than 10 years! They were not really going out of business, but knew people love a bargain and would visit the store thinking they were getting a good deal. Many of the items marked down 50% could be purchased down the street at a lower price.

One aspect of the gift of the Spirit is self-control. Pray that this gift might manifest in your life, and you will not have to worry about controlling your impulse to buy.

Assignment

- Record in your journal the fresh insights God gives you as you meditate on this lesson.
- Have you ever purchased anything on impulse? How did that work out for you?
- Do you feel this is a serious problem in the church today?
- What can the church do to help combat impulse buying?

Lesson Twelve - Money Centered Life

There is an old Broadway song...money makes the world go around...and in many ways that is true. However, the bible states that, though money in and of itself is not evil, the love of money is the root of all types of evil. A person whose whole life is consumed with obtaining money and things has wrong priorities.

> *Ecclesiastes 5:10, He who loves money will not be satisfied with money, nor he who loves abundance with its income. This too is vanity.*

If your life is centered on money and material things, you will never be satisfied, nor ever have enough. I read that billionaire Howard Hughes was asked when he would have enough money. His reply was, "when I have one more dollar." His life was centered on making more and more, but in fact, Howard Hughes was never satisfied, and died a very sick and strange old man.

> *Haggai 1:4, "Is it time for you yourselves to dwell in your paneled houses while this house lies desolate?"*

The prophet Haggai warned the people of God that their priorities were back to front. Their focus was on their own property to the neglect of the house of God. Of course, it is certainly ok for us to have houses and cars, and the nice things that the Lord provides, but our priority must always be God's kingdom, for truly only what is done for Christ will last.

> *Matthew 6:24, "No one can serve two masters; for either he will hate the one and love the other, or he will be devoted to one and despise the other. You cannot serve God and wealth.*

So the question which must be asked is "Who is your master?" It cannot be God and money. If your life is centered on money you will not be able to serve God with your whole heart; you have divided loyalties. Money is nothing more than a tool we use in serving God. We should treat it like any other tool.

> *Mark 10:21-26, Looking at him, Jesus felt a love for him and said to him, "One thing you lack: go and sell all you possess and give to the poor, and you will have treasure in heaven; and come, follow Me." But at these words he was saddened, and he went away grieving, for he was one who owned much property. And Jesus, looking around, said to His disciples, "How hard it will be for those who are wealthy to enter the kingdom of God!" The disciples were amazed at His words. But Jesus answered again and said to them, "Children, how hard it is to enter the kingdom of God! It is easier for a camel to go through the eye of a needle than for a rich man to enter the kingdom of God." They were even more astonished and said to Him, "Then who can be saved?"*

Imagine, this young man was being given the opportunity to be with Jesus. He was asked to do the same thing the other disciples were asked to do, leave all to follow Jesus. Unlike the disciples, he chose material possessions over a personal relationship with Jesus. Who knows, if he had accepted he may have been numbered with the Apostles. Do not allow material possessions to keep you from close fellowship with Jesus.

It is hard for those who trust in riches to give them up to follow Jesus. Jesus did not say it was impossible for a rich person to be saved he simply said it was difficult. God warned the Israelites not to forget Him when they became blessed in the Promised Land. The issue is not money, but who or what you worship and trust in.

> *Luke 9:25, For what is a man profited if he gains the whole world, and loses or forfeits himself?*

You can gain the whole world and lose your very soul if your life revolves around money. Riches cannot be taken with us to heaven.

Why waste your life on the reckless pursuit of money when it does not have eternal value.

> *Luke 12:19-21, And I will say to my soul, "Soul, you have many goods laid up for many years to come; take your ease, eat, drink and be merry."' But God said to him, 'You fool! This very night your soul is required of you; and now who will own what you have prepared?' So is the man who stores up treasure for himself, and is not rich toward God."*

The accumulation of material goods does not insure you a long life. Money cannot stop death. It is better to lay up treasures in heaven than to lay up treasures on earth. Of course, prepare for the future, but also get your priorities right. God always comes first; or at least he should.

> *Philippians 3:18-19, For many walk, of whom I often told you, and now tell you even weeping, that they are enemies of the cross of Christ, whose end is destruction, whose god is their appetite, and whose glory is in their shame, who set their minds on earthly things.*

Those who set their minds on earthly things are enemies of the cross. Their end is destruction and their god is their belly and their glory is shame. When you serve money you become an enemy to God. God is a jealous god and He will share His glory with no other god. It is easy to have jealousy over those who seem to have life made. Don't become jealous…God knows your journey and will provide all you need to fulfill your purpose. Sometimes we look at those we think are living the "good life" and we become jealous of their riches. Remember to put your trust in God and not in money.

> *1 Timothy 6:10, For the love of money is a root of all sorts of evil, and some by longing for it have wandered away from the faith and pierced themselves with many griefs.*

The love of money is the root of all types of evil. Note it does say money is evil, but the love of money is evil. There is nothing wrong with having money as long as your life is not controlled by it. Our love should be directed toward God and God alone.

> *2 Timothy 3:1-5, But realize this, that in the last days difficult times will come. For men will be lovers of self, lovers of money, boastful, arrogant, revilers, disobedient to parents, ungrateful, unholy, unloving, irreconcilable, malicious gossips, without self-control, brutal, haters of good, treacherous, reckless, conceited, lovers of pleasure rather than lovers of God, holding to a form of godliness, although they have denied its power; Avoid such men as these.*

> *1 John 2:15-16, Do not love the world nor the things in the world. If anyone loves the world, the love of the Father is not in him. For all that is in the world, the lust of the flesh and the lust of the eyes and the boastful pride of life, is not from the Father, but is from the world.*

You cannot love both God and the world system. God never tells us not to have the things of the world because He knows we need them to exist. His warning is about a love for them. This is a heart issue and not a money one. Where does the true affection of our heart rest – with God or stuff.

Assignment

- Record in your journal the fresh insights God gives you as you meditate on this lesson.
- Give examples of times you have seen the love of money hinder someone's walk.
- Do you feel this is a big issue in the church today?
- How can this impact this church?

Lesson Thirteen - Surety (Co-signing)

Proverbs 6:1-5, My son, if you have become surety for your neighbor, have given a pledge for a stranger, If you have been snared with the words of your mouth, have been caught with the words of your mouth, Do this then, my son, and deliver yourself; Since you have come into the hand of your neighbor, go, humble yourself, and importune your neighbor. Give no sleep to your eyes, nor slumber to your eyelids; Deliver yourself like a gazelle from the hunter's hand and like a bird from the hand of the fowler.

Many years ago, I (Stan) was asked by a Pastor to help him buy a car. It was a used Mercedes Benz, which looked to be in good shape and indeed would be a good car for the pastor to have. He told me he could handle the payments, but would need to have someone cosign on the loan since his credit was bad, due to no fault of his own, he assured me. I have a big heart and sometimes a soft brain, I agreed…the amount of the loan was $5,000. A few weeks after he bought the car, he allowed his teen son to drive it and he blew up the engine…and the pastor told me he was able to get another car, but could not pay for the one that had been destroyed…nor would he…so, I was stuck with a $5,000 bill…what a lesson!

Proverbs 11:15, He who is guarantor for a stranger will surely suffer for it, but he who hates being a guarantor is secure.

If you become surety (a cosigner) you may very well suffer. Security comes from not having debt. This scripture speaks about debt you incur by signing for a loan with someone else. Many people have gotten into trouble because they trusted a friend and signed a loan for them. As mentioned above, I certainly learned my lesson the hard way!

Proverbs 17:18, A man lacking in sense pledges and becomes guarantor in the presence of his neighbor

Proverbs 22:26-27, Do not be among those who give pledges, among those who become guarantors for debts. If you have nothing with which to pay, why should he take your bed from under you?

Only a man who lacks understanding will become surety for someone else. All wise counsel and Godly wisdom speak against this practice. However, it happens all the time. You stand the chance of losing everything if the other person does not repay the loan. Your family and all you have worked for can be jeopardized by signing a loan for another person...use wisdom!

Assignment

- Record in your journal the fresh insights God gives you as you meditate on this lesson.
- Have you ever cosigned for someone, or anyone for you? How did it work out?
- Is this a major or minor issue in the church today?
- How can this impact the church?

Lesson Fourteen - Withholding Wages

Leviticus 19:13, 'You shall not oppress your neighbor, nor rob him. The wages of a hired man are not to remain with you all night until morning.

When a person works for you it is your responsibility to make sure you pay them what they are owed. There are many cases where people work for long periods of time and they are never paid. When an employer does this it blocks God's blessing in their lives.

Deuteronomy 24:14-15, "You shall not oppress a hired servant who is poor and needy, whether he is one of your countrymen or one of your aliens who is in your land in your towns. You shall give him his wages on his day before the sun sets, for he is poor and sets his heart on it; so that he will not cry against you to the Lord and it become sin in you.

God is on the side of an exploited worker. You do not want God as your enemy, so pay your workers what is due them. This is a big problem in the church in Africa. Many pastors want young men coming up in the ministry to work fulltime for the church, but they refuse to pay them. As a result many of these young men split the church, starting their own ministry so they can survive. This is not God's method of church planting!

Isaiah 30:23-24, Then He will give you rain for the seed which you will sow in the ground, and bread from the yield of the ground, and it will be rich and plenteous; on that day your livestock will graze in a roomy pasture. Also the oxen and the donkeys which work the ground will eat salted fodder, which has been winnowed with shovel and fork.

Your workers are to eat of the increase of their labor. Those who help you make money are to be partakers in what they help you make. Pay them their salaries when it is due. Even the animals who help till the ground eat of the fruit of their labor.

> *Jeremiah 22:13, "Woe to him who builds his house without righteousness and his upper rooms without justice, who uses his neighbor's services without pay and does not give him his wages,*

> *Malachi 3:5, "Then I will draw near to you for judgment; and I will be a swift witness against the sorcerers and against the adulterers and against those who swear falsely, and against those who oppress the wage earner in his wages, the widow and the orphan, and those who turn aside the alien and do not fear Me," says the Lord of hosts.*

God places withholding wages in the same light as adultery and perjury, and those who exploit orphans and widows. God has his ways of making things right.

> *Matthew 10:9-10, Do not acquire gold, or silver, or copper for your money belts, or a bag for your journey, or even two coats, or sandals, or a staff; for the worker is worthy of his support.*

Jesus told the disciples when they went to preach the Gospel they would be taken care of by those they ministered to. We have an obligation to take care of those who give us the word of God.

> *Luke 10:7, Stay in that house, eating and drinking what they give you; for the laborer is worthy of his wages. Do not keep moving from house to house.*

When we preach the gospel we are to live with the people and eat what is offered to us. In my travels around the world I function this way. The churches who host me take care of me to the best of their ability. Like Paul, I am content with what the people are able to afford. Because I bring them the Gospel, I am worthy to be taken care of by the Gospel.

1 Corinthians 9:7, Who at any time serves as a soldier at his own expense? Who plants a vineyard and does not eat the fruit of it? Or who tends a flock and does not use the milk of the flock?

When we work we expect to be compensated for our labor. Not only is this commanded in scripture it is also common sense.

1 Corinthians 9:9-11, For it is written in the Law of Moses, "You shall not muzzle the ox while he is threshing." God is not concerned about oxen, is He? Or is He speaking altogether for our sake? Yes, for our sake it was written, because the plowman ought to plow in hope, and the thresher to thresh in hope of sharing the crops. If we sowed spiritual things in you, is it too much if we reap material things from you?

Workers are to be partakers of the fruit of their labor. The ox can eat while he is helping to thresh the grain. Again workers need to be paid for their labor.

1 Corinthians 9:14, So also the Lord directed those who proclaim the gospel to get their living from the gospel.

James 5:4, Behold, the pay of the laborers who mowed your fields, and which has been withheld by you, cries out against you; and the outcry of those who did the harvesting has reached the ears of the Lord of Sabaoth.

Not only will the workers cry out to God but their very wages will testify against you. God is serious about the withholding of wages for worthy workers.

Assignment

- Record in your journal the fresh insights God gives you as you meditate on this lesson.
- Give examples of times you have been confronted with this blockade.

- How did you respond at the time?
- How would you respond now as a result of this lesson?
- Do you feel this is a big issue in the church today?
- How can this impact the church?

Lesson Fifteen - Wrong Priorities

Many times the flow of God's blessings are slowed down or stopped because we have wrong priorities in our lives and ministries. Presented here is a brief discussion of the proper priorities for the life of a believer.

1st Priority - GOD

Matthew 6:33, But seek first His kingdom and His righteousness, and all these things will be added to you.

God knows what we need before we even know we have a need. He is willing to meet every need when we seek Him first. It is our responsibility to seek His will and plan before anything else. There is no higher calling in life than knowing God, and we know Him by seeking Him.

Proverbs 3:9-10, Honor the Lord from your wealth and from the first of all your produce; so your barns will be filled with plenty and your vats will overflow with new wine.

If you honor God first, He will bless you. Paying our tithes and offerings is a way to bring honor to God and put Him first. Possessions are simply tools to help us serve God. We must guard our hearts so God always comes before our things. There are many people who serve things and the accumulation of wealth takes priority over all else. For the believer this should never be the case. There is nothing wrong with wealth as long as they are used as tools for serving God.

Psalms 146:3-5, Do not trust in princes, in mortal man, in whom there is no salvation. His spirit departs, he returns to the earth; in that very day his thoughts perish. How blessed is he whose help is the God of Jacob, whose hope is in the Lord his God.

God will never let you down. If you prioritize the help of a man before God, you are setting yourself up for a great disappointment. People will fail you. God never does. When a friend asks you to do something, check with God to see if it is the right thing to do. When God says to do something, you don't need to ask your friend if it is the right thing to do, just do it!

> Deuteronomy 6:12, ...then watch yourself, that you do not forget the LORD who brought you from the land of Egypt, out of the house of slavery.

Always remember it is God who blesses us with all good things. We need to remind ourselves that everything we have comes from God. Sometimes we think we accomplished some great thing for God out of our own strength. The reality is it is only with God's help and protection we are able to accomplish anything. Without God we are nothing. One of my mentors will look at me, shake his head and say, "Did you ever think a farm boy from Louisiana would do what you are doing for God?" This simple statement helps me to refocus on God and what He has done; rather than deceiving myself that I did some great thing. God must always come first.

2nd Priority – ESSENTIALS

The essentials of life are food and water, shelter and clothing. These are the things needed to maintain life. Further, it is our families and their relationships that are essential.

> 1 Timothy 5:8, But if anyone does not provide for his own, and especially for those of his household, he has denied the faith and is worse than an unbeliever.

It is sad when we see men of God in the ministry put the ministry above their families. Once I was taking a young man in our ministry on a trip with me. When he arrived at the airport I asked him if he had left enough money with his wife to take care of the family while he was gone. His response was he brought all the money they had with him for the trip, and would believe God to take care of the family. I cancelled his trip: he must take care of his family first and believe God to take care of his needs on the trip. How easy it is to get our priorities out of line.

3rd Priority - NON-ESSENTIALS

The third priority after God and the Essentials of life is to take care of the non-essentials. The non-essentials are things like education for our children, ministry, transportation, recreation and entertainment.

The education of our children should come before the ministry. God has given us children and expects us to take care of them, provide for them and see they have every opportunity to fulfill their destiny. Again, I have seen pastors take the money for their children's education and put it into the ministry because there was a great need. But our children should not needlessly suffer due to our ministry requirements.

Assignment

- Record in your journal the fresh insights God gives you as you meditate on this lesson.
- Give examples of times you have been confronted with setting Wrong Priorities.
- How did you respond at the time?
- How would you respond now as a result of this lesson?
- Do you feel this is a big issue in the church today?
- How can this impact this church?

Lesson Sixteen - Spend Wisely

Money is a tool to be used, not just something to be collected. Learn to use this tool and you will prosper. The wise use of money is as important as having money. There are many people who make a lot of money but have nothing to show for it because they are not wise in their use of their money.

God has called us to be faithful (wise) stewards of the things He has given to us. The wise use of money has little to do with the amount of money we have. You can have five cents and use it wisely or unwisely as easily as if you had millions. The wise use of money comes from allowing the Holy Spirit to be in control. Always ask the Holy Spirit to guide you in the use of your money.

Economize

Buy wisely. Shop around for the best possible price. Do research before making major purchases or investments. By doing the research you learn the specifics of the product and have time to think about what you want and need. Often our wants and our needs are totally different. Research allows you to buy the best product at the best price.

Get the most for your money. Sometimes the cheapest is not the best value. The old saying, "You get what you pay for," is often true. My family was traveling in the United States and I was trying to practice this principle. The problem was I did not do the proper research before buying the cheapest tickets I could find. The airline we flew was late causing us to miss our connections. This resulted in having to pay for a hotel room in for the night. On the return trip they lost all of our luggage. In this case the cheapest ticket was not the best value, as I ended up spending more on hotel rooms and food than I saved on the cheap ticket.

Jesus taught this principle in the feeding of the 5000. They collected everything left over so nothing was wasted. I do not want to stand before Jesus on judgment day to discover I was not a good steward of the things He gave me.

Assignment

- Record in your journal the fresh insights God gives you as you meditate on this lesson.
- Give examples of times you have not spent your money wisely.
- How did you respond at the time?
- How would you respond now as a result of this lesson?
- Do you feel this is a big issue in the church today?
- How can this impact this church?

Lesson Seventeen - Living Debt Free

There are two types of debt. One is really an appreciating asset, such as a house. You may buy off a house with a loan, but if it is worth more than you owe, it is an asset. However, revolving credit, such as with credit cards, costs many times more to service than the amount borrowed. This type of debt can strangle a family.

Here are 13 steps to conquering debt so you can focus on what really matters.

- Ask God: Seek God's wisdom for overcoming financial bondage. Jesus had more to say about money than He did any other subject.
- Budget: Sure, it seems like a no-brainer, but there is nothing as revealing as a personal budget to account for income and outlay of household finances. (Note: the next section shows how to make a budget)
- List debts and interest: Starting with small balances first, use any unexpected income to pay down your debt
- Get outside assistance: Find a financial adviser who understands your values as a Christian to help you map out a plan for financial freedom
- Practice full disclosure: Do not hide financial trouble from your spouse. Seek his or her advice, and bear the load together.
- Deprive yourself: Stop spending for things you can do without. One idea: Agree not to make any major consumer purchases for at least two years.
- Become content: Credit-card debt is often accrued from purchasing unnecessary items on an impulse. Until this behavioral habit is adjusted, a financial plan will be of little help.
- Consider using a debit card: This gives the convenience of a credit card, but utilizes assets you already have.

- Consider temporary discontinuing contributions to savings or retirement: It does not make sense to receive 7 percent on your investment while you are paying 18 percent on debt.
- Live on less than you earn: Then take the balance and begin to repay debt and start a savings account.
- Keep track of cash from ATMs: Cash is not called liquid by accident. Account for even small purchases in your budget, so you can track spending.
- Discontinue any purchases that are not absolutely essential: Live with it, do it yourself, repair it, or do without.
- Reduce your credit-card selection to one card: Avoid special use cards. Get an all-purpose card and pay off the balance at the end of each month.[1]

Assignment

- Record in your journal the fresh insights God gives you as you meditate on this lesson.
- Give examples of times you have been in debt in the past.
- How did you respond at the time?
- How would you respond now as a result of this lesson?
- Do you feel this is a big issue in the church today?
- How can this impact this church?

---

[1] Clements, Patrick L. Financial Freedom: More Than Being Debt Free, VMI Publishers

Lesson Eighteen - How to Make a Budget

Set up Budget Categories, Calculate Budget Amounts

Without a budget, many of us simply stay one step ahead of our bills. If the word "budget" makes you cringe, think of the process as (1) summarizing how you spend your income and (2) creating guidelines for your spending. No blame, no shame, no deprivation, and no guilt. Thinking of a budget as a financial diet is a sure way to set yourself up for failure. A budget is simply (1) a tool to increase your consciousness of how and where you spend your money, and (2) a guideline to help you spend your money on the things that are most important to you.

Step One: Set Up Categories

The first step is establishing income and expense categories to track. A common mistake is to fit your spending into somebody else's categories. While basic categories such as housing, utilities, insurance, and food apply to all of us, we each have expenses that are unique to our personal situation.

A successful budget will include categories which reflect the way YOU actually spend money.

For example, if you regularly eat lunch out at work, you'll want a subcategory under "Food" for "Lunches Out." Think about your hobbies (golfing, crafts, gardening) and your habits (buying a cup of coffee every day, reading the daily paper) to identify other spending categories. The idea is to become more aware of where your money goes so you can make conscious decisions about spending.

If it helps to start with a budget worksheet, there are many available in books and online, but be sure to add and delete categories to customize the worksheet to your needs.

Step Two: Calculate Budget Amounts

To get started, collect as many of your pay stubs, bills, and receipts as possible. Calculate your average monthly gross pay (before taxes) by adding the gross pay on four pay stubs if you're paid weekly, or two pay stubs if you're paid twice a month. If your pay varies substantially from pay period to pay period, try to come up with as accurate a monthly average as possible. Now do the same for any interest income, dividends, bonuses, or other miscellaneous income.

Next, start reviewing your bills for at least the last three months and listing monthly expenses on a budget worksheet (see "Basic Budget Worksheet" in Appendix 1). Make your categories detailed enough to provide you with useful information about your spending habits, but not so detailed you become bogged down in trivial details. Remember, this has to be something you'll stick with for the long term, so you don't want it to be too much of a chore.

To determine your monthly budgeted amounts for each category, it's important to walk a fine line between realistically reflecting your actual expenses and setting targeted spending levels which will enable you to save money. Even fixed costs such as housing or utilities can often be reduced. Start out by reviewing your bills from the last several months, and entering monthly budgeted amounts for each category. Later, when you have a better grasp on your spending, you'll look for ways to reduce many of these expenses.[2]

Remember, the budget worksheet in the appendix is only a worksheet. Be sure to make adjustments to fit your lifestyle and spending habits. This is your budget so make it work for you. If it does not work to help you make better use of your money then you will not stick with it.

---

[2]   http://financialplan.about.com/cs/budgeting/a/GuiltFreeBudget.htm

Assignment

- Record in your journal the fresh insights God gives you as you meditate on this lesson.
- Work on making a practical budget for yourself.

Lesson Nineteen - Sowing and Reaping

Where it Began

Man in the Garden of Eden was completely provided for the same way God fed the animals. He did not have to work or worry about his needs being supplied. God was his provider for everything. Sin brought the curse of God upon earth and man. As a result of sin man was forced out of the garden of Eden and God instituted a new principle upon man: The principle of SOWING AND REAPING.

Scriptures on Sowing and Reaping

2 Corinthians 9:6 – 11, Now this I say, he who sows sparingly will also reap sparingly, and he who sows bountifully will also reap bountifully. Each one must do just as he has purposed in his heart, not grudgingly or under compulsion, for God loves a cheerful giver. And God is able to make all grace abound to you, so that always having all sufficiency in everything, you may have an abundance for every good deed; as it is written,

"HE SCATTERED ABROAD, HE GAVE TO THE POOR, HIS RIGHTEOUSNESS ENDURES FOREVER."

Now He who supplies seed to the sower and bread for food will supply and multiply your seed for sowing and increase the harvest of your righteousness; you will be enriched in everything for all liberality, which through us is producing thanksgiving to God.

There is much in the Word of God about sowing and reaping. We will only look at a few scriptures for a firm foundation.

Genesis 8:22, "While the earth remains, Seedtime and harvest, And cold and heat, And summer and winter, And day and night Shall not cease."

The principle of sowing and reaping will remain as long as the earth remains. God has placed sowing and reaping as a reminder of the consequences of sin and disobedience to His word.

> *Luke 6:38, "Give, and it will be given to you. They will pour into your lap a good measure—pressed down, shaken together, and running over. For by your standard of measure it will be measured to you in return."*

Each person determines the size of their harvest at the moment of their giving. This lesson was taught to me growing up on a farm. My father determined the size of his harvest by the amount of ground he prepared and the amount of seed he planted. If you can prepare 100 acres but only plant 10 acres you will get a 10 acre crop. On the other hand, if you prepare 10 acres and plant 100 acres you will still only get a 10 acre harvest because the seed will not grow in unprepared ground.

We purpose in our hearts beforehand the way we should give. Do not be stingy in sowing your seed (giving) because the way you sow will determine the size of your harvest. God loves it when His people give with a cheerful heart. Some people look like they are about to have a tooth pulled when it is time to give an offering. Determine what you will give and the attitude you will have before you give.

> *Galatians 6:7 – 10, Do not be deceived, God is not mocked; for whatever a man sows, this he will also reap. For the one who sows to his own flesh will from the flesh reap corruption, but the one who sows to the Spirit will from the Spirit reap eternal life. Let us not lose heart in doing good, for in due time we will reap if we do not grow weary. So then, while we have opportunity, let us do good to all people, and especially to those who are of the household of the faith.*

Understand, God knows our heart. Some people seem to think God can be tricked into blessing them. We will reap what we sow. From all our years of farming we never once saw corn come from a bean seed or beans come from wheat seed. Every time we put a certain type of seed in the ground it was that type of seed we harvested. What you reap is determined by what you sow.

Harvest is not Immediate

You must be diligent, working hard to make sure the seed sown has the best chance to bring a harvest. The farmer will till the ground, apply fertilizer, water the crop and cultivate the crop. With his best effort he cannot guarantee the seed planted will produce a harvest. God is the only one who can bring forth a harvest from seed planted.

It is the same way with financial seed. We must ensure we have done everything we can to provide the best opportunity for our seed to produce a harvest. Research must be done to see if the ground we are planting in is good soil; that it has been productive in the past. The seed must be watered and cultivated through prayer. After we have done all we can, we trust God to give the increase.

A farmer knows there is a gap of time between the planting of seed and the harvest. This is a time of faith, knowing it is all in God's hand. God is the master gardener, so put your trust in Him to bring the harvest in due season.

Assignment

- Record in your journal the fresh insights God gives you as you meditate on this lesson.
- Give examples of times you have seen the results of sowing and reaping.
- How can this impact this church?

Lesson Twenty - Types of Givers

In the late 70s, I heard a great missionary statesman, Danny Ost, give a wonderful teaching on the different types of givers. Here is what he had to say about the way people give to God.

Tippers

Tippers give to God when He does something good for them, or they had a good time at church. If the Pastor was exceptionally good at preaching that day they leave a tip for the good service.

Impulse Givers

Impulse givers give when the urge hits them. Suddenly they feel like giving. Maybe the wife cooked a really good meal and they are happy their child did well on an exam, so they drop some money in the offering plate. Unfortunately, the urge does not hit often.

Legalistic Givers

Legalistic givers give only because they are commanded to give. They would rather not give, but they are afraid of what could happen to them if they do not give. They begrudge God for everything they are forced to give. When it is time to give they look like they have been sucking on lemons.

Emotional Givers

Emotional givers give when an emotional appeal is made for money. A sad story of poverty is told or a missionary shows pictures of destitute children and their emotions are stirred. Maybe the pastor tells how the bills will not be paid and they will have to shut down some program if the people do not give. Appeals like this are made by television and by radio ministers. Because emotions have been stirred people give out of a since of guilt. They feel guilt and shame for not giving like they know they should. Most offerings in our churches are given by emotion. That is why offerings are up and down.

Biblical Givers

Biblical givers understand God is the one who has given all good gifts. They desire to bless God by giving back to Him a small part of what He has given them. These people give out of a willing and thankful heart, because of their love for God. They are generous givers, with their time, talent and treasure.

Assignment

- Record in your journal the fresh insights God gives you as you meditate on this lesson.
- What type of giver are you?
- What steps will you take to become a Biblical giver?

Appendix I

Basic Budget Worksheet

CATEGORY	MONTHLY BUDGET AMOUNT	MONTHLY ACTUAL AMOUNT	DIFFERENCE
INCOME:			
Wages and Bonuses			
Interest Income			
Investment Income			
Miscellaneous Income			
Income Subtotal			
TAXES:			
Federal Tax			
State & Local Tax			
Social Security Tax			
Income Taxes Subtotal			
Spendable Income			
EXPENSES:			
HOME:			
Mortgage or Rent			
Insurance			
Property Taxes			
Repairs/Maintenance			
Improvements			
UTILITIES:			
Electricity			
Water and Sewer			
Natural Gas or Oil			
Telephone (Land Line, Cell)			

FOOD:			
Groceries			
Eating Out, Lunches, Snacks			
FAMILY OBLIGATIONS:			
Child Support			
Alimony			
Education			
Day Care, Babysitting			
HEALTH AND MEDICAL:			
Insurance			
Medical Expenses not covered by insurance			
Fitness			
TRANSPORTATION:			
Car Payments			
Gasoline/Oil			
Repairs/Maintenance/Fees			
Auto Insurance			
Other Transportation (tolls, bus, subway, taxis)			
DEBT PAYMENTS:			
Credit Cards			
Loans			
ENTERTAINMENT RECREATION:			
Cable TV/Videos/Movies			
Computer Expense			
Hobbies			
Subscriptions and Dues			
Vacations			

PETS:			
Food			
Grooming, Boarding, Vet			
CLOTHING:			
INVESTMENTS AND SAVINGS:			
401(K)or IRA			
Stocks/Bonds/Mutual Funds			
College Fund			
Savings			
Emergency Fund			
MISCELLANEOUS:			
Toiletries, Household Products			
Gifts/Donations			
Grooming (Hair, Make-up, Other)			
Miscellaneous Expense			
Total Investments and Expenses			
Surplus or Shortage (Spendable income minus total expenses and investments)			

Appendix II - Teaching Outlines on Finances

The following is a collection of sermon notes I have preached over the years or I have heard others preach. Please feel free to use these outlines in your church or ministry.

I. The Tithe

What is the tithe?

1. 10% of your increase (profit)
   a. Greek- dekate – a tenth part of anything
   b. Hebrew- ma`aser- a tenth part
      - Payment of a tenth part
2. God's portion of what He has blessed us with
3. Deuteronomy 16:17 – You give to God according to the blessing of the Lord
4. Mark 12:43, 44 – Giving out of your livelihood, not out of what you have left over
5. Genesis 28:22 – It is one tenth of all God gives to you

When did it begin?

1. Before the law
2. Genesis 14:18-20 – With Abraham
3. Genesis 28:22 – Jacob

The tithe is Holy unto the Lord

Leviticus 27:30-33 – From the Old Testament – If you borrowed from it you must pay it back with 20% interest

Tithing is an Act of Worship

Deuteronomy 26:2, 10 – Bring the first fruits to the house of God and worship before the Lord

Philippians 4:14-18 – our offerings are a sweet smelling sacrifice offered to God.

- When you give your money to God it is giving a part of yourself to Him in worship

Tithing is a Sign of the Covenant

Deuteronomy 8:18 – God gives us power to get wealth so His covenant will be established.

Where does the Tithe Go?

1. To Jesus – Genesis 14:18-20 and Hebrews 5:6
2. To the Church – Malachi 3:10
3. To the Leadership – Acts 4:34-35

What is it used for?

1. Running the local church – Malachi 3:10
2. Helping widows, orphans, and the poor – Acts 20:35
3. Outreach ministries – 1 Timothy 6:17,18

When do we Pay our Tithe?

1. Proverbs 3:9 – as soon as you get money
2. 1 Corinthians 16:2 – Every Sunday

How do we Pay our Tithe?

1. You are to bring your tithe to the church
   a. Malachi 3:10
   b. 2 Chronicles 31:5
2. Bring it with rejoicing
   a. Deuteronomy 12:6
   b. 2 Corinthians 9:7
3. Bring it with simplicity, without a show
   a. Matthew 6:3-4
4. Bring it freely, abundantly, willingly
   a. Matthew 10:8
   b. Exodus 35:5
   c. Exodus 35:29
   d. Exodus 36:5-6 this shows the results

Where is Tithing in the New Testament?

1. Jesus taught about tithing
   a. Matthew 23:23
   b. Look at Luke 18:11-12 and compare it with Matthew 5:20
2. Paul taught about tithing (or generous giving... at least tithing)
   a. Romans 4:12
   b. Romans 4:16
   c. Compare 1 Corinthians 9:7-14 and 1 Timothy 6: 17-18

What are the Blessings of Tithing?

1. Malachi 3:10-11 – God will open the windows of heaven and he will rebuke the devourer
2. Proverbs 3:10 – You will have abundant harvests
3. Proverbs 11:25 – Your soul will be fat and you will be watered
4. Matthew 10:42 – You will receive a reward
5. Matthew 14:15-21 – What you give will be multiplied and used to bless many people
6. 1 Chronicles 29:13-17 – We become co-workers with God
7. Acts 20:35 – More blessed to give than receive.
8. 1 Timothy 6:10 – Develops a spirit of generosity.
9. Matthew 6:20 – We lay up treasure in heaven.
10. Matthew 6:33 – All our needs are met,
11. It allows every believers an opportunity to share in the work of God on an equal basis

II. Stewardship

What is a steward?

Genesis 39:3-4 – one who manages another's property, finances, or other affairs. He is an administrator or supervisor. Joseph was the steward in the house of Potiphar.

A steward was usually a trusted servant who looked after the affairs of his master.

Stewardship is what you do with what God has entrusted to you.

Parable of the Unjust Steward (Luke 16:1-13)

1. Overview of this parable

It teaches faithfulness in financial matters will make a person worthy of trust by God in spiritual matters.

We must make the best use of what God has given us in this world.

If we are to act wisely, we must be as diligent and industrious to use the money God has given to us for the advancement of the kingdom of Heaven, as worldly men are in using money to advance their own causes.

2. "Which had a steward" (v1)

We are all stewards of God

All we have belongs to God and He has allowed us use of it for a short while.

3. "give account of your stewardship" (v2)

Every person will have to stand before God and give an account of what he did with the things God put in his trust.

Money is the least important thing we have to account for.

We must account for our WORDS (Matthew 12:36-37)

We must account for our WORKS (Matthew 16:27)

We must account for our LIVES (Romans 14:12-13)

We must account for our MINISTRY (1 Corinthians 3:8, 13-15)

To avoid the judgement of God as an unjust steward we must:

    1. IMPROVE that which has been entrusted to us or

2. INCREASE what was entrusted to us or
3. USE what was entrusted to us for its proper use

4. "and I say to you" (v9)

Jesus makes the application of this parable to his disciples. It was not enough for them to hear a word from Jesus, they must be able to apply that word to their own lives.

"unrighteous mammon"

1. things that will one day perish
2. it will always disappoint the one who trusts in it

Though unrighteous mammon cannot be looked to for help or happiness we are to make proper use of it.

The men of this world will know how to:

1. Manage money so it will benefit from now
2. Invest for future benefits as well
3. Use principles of finance and good money management

WE SHOULD LEARN from them to make use of money and the resources we have so we may see the Gospel spread and also lay up treasures for ourselves in heaven.

WE MUST BE CAREFUL STEWARDS of this world's goods so when we die we may be received into an eternal habitation with our God.

5. "he that is faithful" (v10)

It is NOT THE AMOUNT that has been given to us BUT OUR STEWARDSHIP of it that matters to God.

We must get into the habit of being faithful in the smallest things if we ever expect God to trust us with greater things.

1) a man who will steal one shilling will steal one million if he is given the chance

2) a man who is trustworthy with one shilling can be trusted with one million

6. **"if ye therefore have not been faithful (v11)**

    a. unrighteous mammon
       1) not trusted in money matters
       2) improper use of things given
    b. true riches of God
       1) Wisdom of God
       2) Gifts of the Holy Spirit
       3) Anointing of the Spirit
       4) Revelation from God's Word
       5) Ministry to God's people
    c. If you cannot trust a man in your church with the church's money then do not trust him with the spiritual matters of the church.

7. **"and if you have not been faithful in that which is another man's" (v12)**

If God cannot trust us with the riches that belong to another person how can we expect him to give us riches of our own.

If we are not faithful to another man's ministry God will never give us ministry.

The Parable of the Talents (Matthew 25:14-30)

    1. God is our source of supply (v14-15)

       a. He is Jehovah-Jireh, our provider
       b. We must put our trust in Him (not our jobs) to supply our needs
       c. God alone is responsible for the increase in the seed we have sown.

2. We must be good stewards (v16-23)

   a. Use what was given us for the proper use to see an increase in the Kingdom
   b. We must be willing to use what God has given us.
   c. Be a channel of God's blessings like the Sea of Galilee and not like the Dead Sea.
   d. If we make proper use of what God has given us then more will be given to us and we can enter into the joy of the Lord.

3. Don't be afraid of God (v24-27)

This man was afraid he would do the wrong thing with what he was given so he did nothing.

This man put the blame for his own slothfulness on his master.

Because he did not use what was given to him he lost it.

His wickedness was not that he did some terrible thing against his master, but he did nothing for his master.

He said to himself, "I cannot do much so I will do nothing. No one would notice the little I had to offer anyway"

Rewards and Punishments (v28-30)

If you are faithful with the little you have you will be blessed, rewarded and given even more.

If you are unfaithful you will be punished and the little you have will be taken away.

Charles Spurgeon said, "We all have talent. It may be only one, but we are *responsible* for it. Are we acting up to the measure of our ability? Many wish they had more talents, but this wrong, for the Lord has entrusted us with quite as many talents as he can give a soul. Our great concern should be to be found faithful steward of such things as we have."

Be concerned for what you have now and stop worrying about what you wish God would give you.

3. Financial Responsibility and Accountability

1 Corinthians 4:2 – Responsibility

We are required to use our material goods justly and wisely for the furtherance of the Kingdom of God.

The wrong use of money placed in our hands can completely destroy our testimony and usefulness in the Kingdom,

The most spiritual thing a person can do to promote their usefulness in the Kingdom is to be a responsible steward of the things God has given to them.

We should strive to have the testimony by every man (sinner and saint) that we are honest.

2 Corinthians 8:20-21 – Accountability

We as stewards of God are accountable to both God and Man.

Many ministries have suffered because people were not willing to give an accounting to God or to men for the finances which were given to them.

Unwillingness to give accountability suggests the person in question is guilty of some wrongdoing they are trying to hide.

Not being accountable for finances leads to a lack of trust by others.

Keep good records and be willing to let people look at your records to see for themselves how you are using the money that has been given to you.

4. Finances and the Local Church

God wants every local church to be self-supporting (Acts 2:44-47)

By the tithes of its members.
By the free will gifts above the tithe of its members.

God does not need or want Harambees to build His church. He wants His people to give. You have not given God until you give above and beyond the tithe because Leviticus 27:30 tells us that the tithe already belongs to the Lord. If you are keeping something that belongs to another person and then you return it to them, you have not really given them anything but only returned what you were keeping to the rightful owner. It is the same with the tithe.

God wants the members to have their needs met

1. Acts 2:45 – Everyone shared with those in need.
2. Acts 4:34-35 – The Apostles gave to those in need.
3. Galatians 6:10 – We are to do good to all, especially those in the church.

Every member is responsible to finance the church programs

1 Corinthians 16:2 – Lay something aside as the Lord prospers you.

2 Corinthians 9:7 – Give as you purpose in your heart to give, willingly and cheerfully.

Malachi 3:10 – Bring your tithes so there will be plenty for church programs.

God is looking to every member to give accordingly to what he has. A record should be kept of what each person gives during the year. This will help leadership know who is tithing and will encourage the people when they see how much they gave in a year.

The Leadership is Responsible for the Finances

Acts 4:35 – The offerings were brought to the Apostles to distribute. Acts 6:1-4 – Deacons were appointed to handle the distribution of the offerings.

The leadership is responsible before God as to how they distribute the tithe and offerings of the Church.

The tithes and offerings of the Church go to support the leadership and programs of the church. It only takes people to tithe for the pastor to be supported completely by the church if he is willing to live at the same level of the people.

The Church should tithe of the tithe

Nehemiah 10:38 – To support outreach.

Numbers 18:26-28 – There was to be a tithe of the tithe.

Appendix III – MEDITATION

In modern culture, meditation is often connected with non-Christian systems of thought (examples – yoga, transcendental meditation, New Age, etc.). Christians may at times be uncomfortable with the idea of "meditation," but it is commanded by God and modeled by the godly in Scripture. True meditation is NOT daydreaming. It is NOT allowing our mind to drift here and there. It is NOT thinking about nothing.

True Biblical Meditation:

True Biblical meditation is disciplined thought, and it involves filling your mind with God and His truth (not doing your best to empty the mind).

Biblical meditation requires constructive mental activity (not an attempt to achieve complete mental passivity). Further, it involves focusing on things that are true (Phil. 4:8), linking with prayer to God and responsible, Spirit-filled human action to effect changes (not the "creation of your own reality").

Biblical meditation is "deep thinking on the truths and spiritual realities revealed in Scripture for the purposes of understanding, application, and prayer, and goes far beyond hearing, reading, studying, and even memorizing.

A good analogy - tea bag in water. One dip is merely "reading the Word," "Bible Study," "listening to sermons," etc. Meditation is illustrated by the tea bag left in the water – never taken out.

Joshua 1:18 –

Notice the *"day and night,"* connection between success and practice of meditation on God's Word, our meditation, saturates our conversation and affects action.

Psalm 1:1-3 –

The results of meditation will be stability, fruitfulness, perseverance, and prosperity.

Psalm 119:98-99 –

Developing The Discipline of Meditation

Repeat a phrase or verse in different ways, emphasizing a different word each time.

Example:

I am the resurrection and the life.

I AM the resurrection and the life.

I am the RESURRECTION and the life.

I am the resurrection and the LIFE.

Rewrite it in your own words. Paraphrase the text, making it personal. Rethink and restate the verse using "you" words in the process.

Look for applications of the text.

How am I to respond to this? What would God have me to do?

Application—chew---then swallow.

Pray through text.

This submits my mind to the Holy Spirit and intensifies spiritual perception.

Don't rush-Take your time! Read LESS (if necessary) in order to meditate MORE.

We are often too impatient. We must sometimes force ourselves to slow down and chew! Only then can we digest properly and grow in sanctified character.

Compare the verse with another Scripture. Reflect on this in relation to two or three other passages. Weave them altogether into your thoughts.

The goal of meditation: **RELATIONSHIP!** To KNOW Jesus intimately! He invites us to "Come unto Me," and He desires to have a deep abiding relationship with us. Just knowing biblical facts will not be enough for this to happen. We must "abide" in Him, and allow His words to abide in us. (John 15:7). Only when this happens will we be "fruitful and multiply." (v.8)

Appendix IV – Spiritual Journaling

Journaling is a powerful key to the development of our spiritual life. As we travel along this journey with Jesus, His Holy Spirit teaches us spiritual insights we have never seen before. We will be experiencing breakthroughs into new levels of maturity. A journal provides a special, private place to express all of our inner thoughts and feelings along the way. Through the process of writing, we understand who we are in Christ and what He has in store for us. An ongoing log of our spiritual development not only provides a great way of measuring our progress, but it can also prove to be a basis of discussion when a mentor meets with his disciple.

Obviously, everyone is different. Some enjoy journaling immensely, and find it to be extremely beneficial and rewarding. Words will literally "flow" from their pens. Others find journaling challenging, finding it difficult to pump out even a few phrases. As a mentor, we must encourage each person to do their best at his or her own particular level. If someone finds journaling difficult, perhaps just a few words will be enough to record what God is doing in their life now. Whatever the case, we are all in process. God is still working on us and we must be careful not to discourage our disciples.

So, how do we get started? Just write! Purchase a notebook/ journal, and keep it with your Bible. Be sure to date each journal entry. This will allow for a quick retrieval of materials that have been previously entered. In your time alone with the Lord, jot down anything the Holy Spirit is "highlighting" for you personally. Below are some suggestions you may find helpful:

- Jot down the answer to this all-important question whenever you read Scripture: How is my life touched today by this passage?
- As you meditate, note any word, phrase, scene, or image that emerges from the passage.

- Record what you sense this passage is calling you to do or be.
- Do not be afraid to mention any feelings, reflections, images, thoughts- just "whatever comes to mind" in your journal.
- Dialogue with the Lord. Sometimes you may want to write your prayers out, and even what you believe the Lord is speaking back to you. (You will be surprised later as to how "right on" these journal entries turn out to be!)
- If you have a question you want to ask the Lord, write it down. Wait on the Lord for the answer- and record it when it comes.
- Record prayer requests and answers
- Be free to pour out your frustrations, emotional pain, confusion, etc., in this journal. God can use this as a path to His healing touch.
- You may want to include timely Bible verses, meaningful quotations, and current lessons you are learning from the Holy Spirit. Be free to note anything that "rings a bell" in your life right now.
- You name it! Write it! You will never regret making this practice of journaling a part of your life. You will find your life will be greatly enriched through the discipline of keeping a spiritual journal.

Appendix V –

The Strategy Be 1, Make 1! Think about it!

If a single person with a message wanted to reach as many people as possible, what would he do? All he would need do would be to make sure he communicated the message clearly to one new person each year. He must do so in such a way the new person will be able to communicate the message to others. The first year there will be only one person and his friend. The second year there will be two people who can teach the message. If these two persons communicate the message to two others, then there will be four after three years. At first glance, this plan sounds unimpressive and seems like it would not have much of an impact, but if you can look at how the numbers grow as time goes on you can see the whole world can be reached in less than 34 years!

I realize these numbers are only theoretical. BUT LET'S THINK BEYOND THE AVERAGE! Let's follow Jesus' commandment and be part of fulfilling His Great Commission. I pray the simple chart below might inspire each one of us with the power of multiplication through discipleship

Year	Number of Disciples	Comment
1	1	Just you
2	2	You and a friend
3	4	One family
4	8	Two families
5	16	Small group
6	32	
7	64	
8	128	Small Church Membership
9	256	
10	512	
11	1,024	Large Church Membership

12	2,048	
13	4,096	Small Town
14	8,196	
15	16,384	
16	32,768	
17	65,536	
18	131,072	
19	262,144	Population of average city
20	524,288	
21	1,048,576	
22	2,097,152	Population of Toronto, Canada
23	4,194,304	
24	8,388,608	
25	16,777,216	
26	33,554,432	Population of Canada
27	67,108,864	
28	134,217,728	
29	268,435,456	
30	536,870,912	Population of North America
31	1,073,741,824	Population of China
32	2,147,483,648	
33	4,294,967,296	Just about everybody
34	8,589,934,592	Much more than the population of the world
35	17,179,869,184	More than one can count

Appendix VI – Proverbs for Living Fruitfully

Proverbs 1:19, So are the ways of everyone who gains by violence; It takes away the life of its possessors.

Proverbs 3:9-10, Honor the LORD from your wealth and from the first of all your produce; So your barns will be filled with plenty and your vats will overflow with new wine.

Proverbs 3:28, Do not say to your neighbor, "Go, and come back, and tomorrow I will give *it*, "When you have it with you.

Proverbs 6:6-8, Go to the ant, O sluggard, Observe her ways and be wise, Which, having no chief, Officer or ruler, Prepares her food in the summer *and* gathers her provision in the harvest.

Proverbs 8:20-21, "I walk in the way of righteousness, In the midst of the paths of justice, to endow those who love me with wealth, that I may fill their treasuries.

Proverbs 10:4-5, Poor is he who works with a negligent hand, but the hand of the diligent makes rich. He who gathers in summer is a son who acts wisely, *but* he who sleeps in harvest is a son who acts shamefully.

Proverbs 10:15, The rich man's wealth is his fortress, The ruin of the poor is their poverty.

Proverbs 11:16, A gracious woman attains honor, and ruthless men attain riches.

Proverbs 11:4, Riches do not profit in the day of wrath, but righteousness delivers from death.

Proverbs 11:6, The righteousness of the upright will deliver them, but the treacherous will be caught by *their own* greed.

Proverbs 11:24, There is one who scatters, and *yet* increases all the more, and there is one who withholds what is justly due, *and yet it results* only in want.

Proverbs 11:26, He who withholds grain, the people will curse him, but blessing will be on the head of him who sells *it*.

Proverbs 11:28, He who trusts in his riches will fall, but the righteous will flourish like the *green* leaf.

Proverbs 13:7, There is one who pretends to be rich, but has nothing; A*nother* pretends to be poor, but has great wealth.

Proverbs 13:11, Wealth *obtained* by fraud dwindles, but the one who gathers by labor increases *it*.

Proverbs 13:8, The ransom of a man's life is his wealth, but the poor hears no rebuke.

Proverbs 13:22, A good man leaves an inheritance to his children's children, and the wealth of the sinner is stored up for the righteous.

Proverbs 14:20, The poor is hated even by his neighbor, but those who love the rich are many.

Proverbs 14:21, He who despises his neighbor sins, but happy is he who is gracious to the poor.

Proverbs 15:6, Great wealth is *in* the house of the righteous, but trouble is in the income of the wicked.

Proverbs 15:16, Better is a little with the fear of the LORD than great treasure and turmoil with it.

Proverbs 16:19, It is better to be humble in spirit with the lowly than to divide the spoil with the proud.

Proverbs 16:20, He who gives attention to the word will find good, and blessed is he who trusts in the LORD.

Proverbs 17:18, A man lacking in sense pledges and becomes guarantor in the presence of his neighbor.

Proverbs 18:9, He also who is slack in his work is brother to him who destroys.

Proverbs 18:11, A rich man's wealth is his strong city, and like a high wall in his own imagination.

Proverbs 18:16, A man's gift makes room for him and brings him before great men.

Proverbs 19:4, Wealth adds many friends, but a poor man is separated from his friend.

Proverbs 19:17, One who is gracious to a poor man lends to the LORD, and He will repay him for his good deed.

Proverbs 20:13, Do not love sleep, or you will become poor; Open your eyes, *and* you will be satisfied with food.

Proverbs 20:15, There is gold, and an abundance of jewels; but the lips of knowledge are a more precious thing.

Proverbs 21:5-6, The plans of the diligent *lead* surely to advantage, but everyone who is hasty *comes* surely to poverty. The acquisition of treasures by a lying tongue is a fleeting vapor, the pursuit of death.

Proverbs 21:13, He who shuts his ear to the cry of the poor will also cry himself and not be answered.

Proverbs 21:17, He who loves pleasure *will become* a poor man; He who loves wine and oil will not become rich.

Proverbs 22:1, A *good* name is to be more desired than great wealth, favor is better than silver and gold.

Proverbs 22:4, The reward of humility *and* the fear of the LORD are riches, honor and life.

Proverbs 22:7, The rich rules over the poor, and the borrower *becomes* the lender's slave.

Proverbs 22:9, He who is generous will be blessed, for he gives some of his food to the poor.

Proverbs 22:16, He who oppresses the poor to make more for himself or who gives to the rich, *will* only *come to* poverty.

Proverbs 22:22-23, Do not rob the poor because he is poor, Or crush the afflicted at the gate; For the LORD will plead their case and take the life of those who rob them.

Proverbs 23:4, Do not weary yourself to gain wealth, cease from your consideration *of it*.

Proverbs 23:5, When you set your eyes on it, it is gone. For *wealth* certainly makes itself wings like an eagle that flies *toward* the heavens.

Proverbs 24:30-34, I passed by the field of the sluggard and by the vineyard of the man lacking sense, and behold, it was completely overgrown with thistles; Its surface was covered with nettles, and its stone wall was broken down. When I saw, I reflected upon it; I looked, *and* received instruction. "A little sleep, a little slumber, little folding of the hands to rest, "Then your poverty will come *as* a robber and your want like an armed man."

Proverbs 25:14, *Like* clouds and wind without rain is a man who boasts of his gifts falsely.

Proverbs 27:24, For riches are not forever, nor does a crown *endure* to all generations.

Proverbs 28:6, Better is the poor who walks in his integrity than he who is crooked though he be rich.

Proverbs 28:13, He who conceals his transgressions will not prosper, but he who confesses and forsakes *them* will find compassion.

Proverbs 28:19-20, He who tills his land will have plenty of food, but he who follows empty *pursuits* will have poverty in plenty. A faithful man will abound with blessings, but he who makes haste to be rich will not go unpunished.

Proverbs 28:24, He who robs his father or his mother and says, "It is not a transgression," Is the companion of a man who destroys.

Proverbs 28:27, He who gives to the poor will never want, but he who shuts his eyes will have many curses.

Proverbs 29:24, He who is a partner with a thief hates his own life; He hears the oath but tells nothing.

Proverbs 30:8-9, Keep deception and lies far from me, Give me neither poverty nor riches; Feed me with the food that is my portion, that I not be full and deny *You* and say, "Who is the LORD?" Or that I not be in want and steal, and profane the name of my God.

www.ingramcontent.com/pod-product-compliance
Lightning Source LLC
LaVergne TN
LVHW021518080426
835509LV00018B/2560